Seven Steps to
'Mentschhood'

How to
Help Your
Child
Become
a Mentsch

An Interactive
Guide
for Parents

Stanley H. Fischman

Seven Steps to "Mentschhood"
How to Help Your Child Become a Mentsch – An Interactive Guide for Parents

Published by Penina Press
Text Copyright © 2012 Stanley Fischman

COVER DESIGN: Shanie Cooper
BOOK DESIGN: Ariel Walden
EDITORIAL AND PRODUCTION DIRECTOR: Daniella Barak
EDITOR: Sara Rosenbaum

Soft Cover ISBN: 978-1-936068-23-4

First edition. Printed in Israel

Distributed by:

Urim Publications
POB 52287
Jerusalem 91521, Israel
Tel: 02.679.7633
Fax: 02.679.7634
urim_pub@netvision.net.il

Lambda Publishers, Inc.
527 Empire Blvd.
Brooklyn, NY 11225, USA
Tel: 718.972.5449
Fax: 718.972.6307
mh@ejudaica.com

www.UrimPublications.com

This book is dedicated

to the memory of

my student

ארן יעקב

בן

דניאל וחיה שרה

Oren Jacob Brandt-Rauf

Who modeled mentschhood

each day we were privileged

to know him

Table of Contents

Foreword   7

Preface: What is a Mentsch?   9

Acknowledgments   13

Introduction: Why Create the Seven Steps to
Mentschhood?   15

Introduction for Parents   19

Introduction for Students   22

User's Guide   24

Step #1: You shall love your fellow man as yourself   25

Step #2: You shall not hate your brother in your heart   39

Step #3: You shall not place a stumbling block
before the blind   57

Step #4: Open your hand to your brother, to your
poor and to the needy in your land   75

Step #5: You shall do what is right and what is good   95

Step #6: The ways of the Torah are ways of pleasantness   111

Step #7: You shall be holy   129

Conclusion: Moving toward Mentschhood   140

Afterword: Some Tips for Parenting Success   142

Foreword

בס"ד

One of the most touching and inspirational stories presented in *Seven Steps to Mentschhood* is the one which tells how the Chafetz Chaim ז"ל brought a young man to the realization of the grandeur and holiness of שבת by his passionate and wistful utterance of the word *"Shabbos!"* followed by his equally passionate and gleeful repetition of the word *"Shabbos!"*

Reading that story calls to mind my thirty-four-year-long close, personal friendship and warm collegial relationship with the author of *Seven Steps to Mentschhood*, Reb Zalman Tzvi (Stanley H.) Fischman. Indeed, viewing the entire book through the lens of my intimate acquaintance with Reb Zalman Tzvi allows me to perceive its inner essence and to hear its implicit whispered message breathed into every printed word. For me, it is as if Reb Zalman Tzvi, Chafetz-Chaim-like, were upliftingly proclaiming one single word repeatedly throughout the book without actually saying it – *"Mentsch! Mentsch!"*

The book presents itself as a genre of its own – a work of moralistic art, gently guiding children, their parents and teachers as they work together through seven real-life steps in the lifelong journey toward becoming a mentsch. As readers progress through the book, "shooting for the moon" in the universe of moral maturity, each bit of growth and progress represents "one small step for man; one giant stride for mankind."

Rabbi CHAIM FEUERMAN, Ed. D.,
Professor of Education, Golda Koschitzky Chair,
Chair, Mendheim Student Teaching and Administrative
Internship Mentoring Program, Azrieli Graduate School of
Jewish Education and Administration, Yeshiva University

Rosh Chodesh Elul, 5770 / August 11, 2010

Preface

What is a Mentsch?

A study of several Yiddish/English dictionaries yields the following definitions of the word *mentsch*: Man, human being, person. Some even add descriptions such as caring, a decent person who can be trusted, upright, honorable, responsible, and mature. Yet no dictionary offers the rich and multifaceted definitions ascribed to this one word by those who are familiar with it.

Before reading any further, perhaps you might like to try an experiment. Ask several people at random how they would define the word "mentsch." Do you think they will give you the same definition? You may, in fact, be quite surprised as to how many differing definitions you might hear.

In preparing this chapter, I asked almost fifty children and adults from all walks of life to define the word mentsch. The following are the results in their own words:

(1) "A practicing Jew."

(2) "Choosing actions based upon what is right/doing the right thing."

(3) "A person with *derech eretz*."

(4) "A person who follows the ways of the Torah."

(5) "A person who does good deeds selflessly."

(6) "An honest, respectful, selfless and helpful person."

(7) "Pleasantness, honesty, selflessness, caring, thoughtfulness, good behavior and chessed."

(8) "Always treating everyone with decency as they would want to be treated."

(9) "Somebody whose kindness is ingrained and whose genuine caring of other people is unconditional."

(10) "A mentsch is someone whom other people see as a mentsch."

(11) "Someone who does the right thing."

(12) "A person with character (who does the right thing even though no one is watching)."

(13) "Somebody who has a heart, and does the right thing even before he is asked."

(14) "A person who is spontaneously kind (who gives respect first)."

(15) "A kind soul."

(16) "Someone who does the right thing and looks out for someone else's feelings."

(17) "Someone with good manners. A caring person."

(18) "Someone who is careful to think before they speak."

(19) "Somebody who treats all others with respect."

(20) "A good, decent person."

(21) "Somebody who treats other people nicely, who behaves with proper etiquette."

(22) "The way you conduct yourself politely, throughout your life, so that people care for you as you care for them."

(23) "A person who behaves right, has good manners and cares for others thereby representing the Jewish religion in a good way."

(24) "A good human being."

(25) "Someone with midot and [who] has respect for other people."

(26) "Somebody who shows the proper example."

(27) "Somebody with good manners, integrity and fine character."

(28) "A good, decent, moral and ethical person."

(29) "A good, decent person who goes out of his way for other people."

(30) "Someone who really thinks about other people and puts other people first."

(31) "A good person who is nice to everyone and always does the right thing."

(32) "Being kind to your friends – don't do something you know is wrong; Doing the right thing."

(33) "A person who has manners and respects the Torah and treats their friends nicely."

(34) "A person with high standards socially, utmost respect – caring, giving – who listens and understands."

(35) "Someone who behaves toward other people and treats other people as he wants to be treated and behaves appropriately and kindly to others."

(36) "A role model of Torah, midos and derech eretz."

(37) "Appropriate people interaction."

(38) "A good person."

(39) "Someone who is kind and considerate."

(40) "Somebody who does the right thing most of the time and tries to be good."

(41) "Someone who does the extraordinary thing – not just the right thing but more."

(42) "A caring *human* being."

(43) "A decent person with good intentions."

(44) "Someone who respects other people and who is responsible and able to make good choices."

(45) "A person who is kind to others, caring, sharing and always there if you need them."

(46) "Someone who acts like a person."

(47) "Someone who acts nicely and knows how to behave in any situation."

(48) "A human being, which is the *tzelem Elokim*."

Taken in its totality, these definitions represent an extraordinary description of desired behavior. Yet, as you might have guessed, no two are exactly alike. This creates a significant challenge for those who wish to learn how to be a mentsch or for those interested in teaching *mentschlich* behavior to young people.

Seven Steps to Mentschhood

Upon closer examination, there is at least one concept that forms a recurring theme: The desirability that a mentsch be someone who tries to behave in the "right way" or do "the right thing." However, as the list itself proves, it is far from clear as to exactly what the "right thing" really means, and, more importantly, how we are to go about doing it.

This is where the *Seven Steps To Mentschhood* can be helpful. The "Seven Steps" are based upon the directives of six *pesukim* from *Chumash* and one from *Mishlei* (Proverbs). They represent an orderly progression designed to provide the student with concrete guidelines for mentsch-like behavior particularly at school. Ultimately, the children learn that it is the Torah that shows us the way.

 The wise person will also be able to apply these Steps to other areas of interpersonal behavior outside the school setting. Without these or other Torah-inspired guidelines, each person would have the overwhelmingly difficult task of determining on his own how a good Jew is supposed to behave. By following the Steps, the sincere student will not only have a clearer definition of "mentschlich" behavior, but also will serve as a Torah role model to others.

> *The formula for growing to be a mentsch, as Hashem desires, is through the study of the Torah and by living that study. Regardless of what avenue of livelihood a person might choose for himself, the Torah never said, become a rav or rosh yeshiva. There is no such injunction in the Torah or in Chazal. All the Torah wants is for you to become a Torah individual – a mentsch.* Rav Mordechai Gifter זצ"ל

Acknowledgements

I wish to thank the following people for their help and support in the production of *Seven Steps to Mentschhood*: Rabbi Chaim Feurman, Ed.D, Rabbi Steven Pruzansky, Judy Lieberman, Edna Krausz, Corinne Paroly, and Eve and Larry Yudelson.

For their support in the dedication of this book, I wish to express my appreciation to the family and friends of Dr. Paul and Sherry Brand-Rauf.

I wish to express my appreciation to the professionals at Urim Publications: Yaacov Peterseil, Acquisitions Director; Daniella Barak, Editorial Production Director; and to my editor, Sara Rosenbaum, for her expertise, and for being such a pleasure to work with.

I wish to express my appreciation to my students at Westchester Day School, who helped me learn and teach the pathways to "Mentschhood."

Finally, I am deeply indebted to my dear wife, Faigi, for her constant help, support, and boundless devotion.

Introduction

Why Create the Seven Steps to Mentschhood?

The *Seven Steps to Mentschhood* program was created in response to an often stated need expressed by parents and schools alike to help guide their children on the path to proper Jewish conduct. It was developed in fourth-grade classrooms over a period of about ten years. It is designed to help school-age children learn to treat one another in a way that is compatible with what is often referred to as *"mentschlichkeit."*

Seven Steps to Mentschhood differs from other character-building and *midot* programs, and is characterized by the following unique elements:

Formal versus Informal

The *Seven Steps to Mentschhood* program strives to respond to some of the shortcomings of formal school-based midot and character-building instruction. These are often academic, based upon classroom instruction, and are frequently disconnected from real-life experience. *Seven Steps to Mentschhood* differs in the following ways:

- The Steps are not based on a listing of desired *midot* and identified values. They are, instead, a collection of Torah-based principles that can be applied to the unlimited range of interpersonal interactions and situations that occur among school children.

- Children are not "tested" with pencil and paper, but demonstrate their success by how well they incorporate the Seven Steps into their daily lives.

- Although they do not require classroom instruction, *Seven Steps to Mentschhood* is focused on discussions that stem from actual, everyday classroom situations. As such, the program can be successfully adopted by teachers for classroom use.

Principle Driven

The Torah selections this program is based upon do not represent a collection of rules but instead serve as seven principles of behavior. Parents and children may reflect upon these principles to assess how successful the child was in responding to relevant situations that arise at school. Over time the child will learn to reflect off of these principles and to make the best choices on his own.

Artificiality versus Reality

Parents frequently express the opinion that school is not the "real world." Yet for children, the classroom and the playing fields are very much the essence of their real world. *Seven Steps to Mentschhood* enables children to explore "real-world" situations, determine how best to apply the Steps and to carry them out successfully when real-life challenges and opportunities present themselves.

Role Modeling

The story is told of Dr. Jonah Folkman who, several years ago, discovered a promising anti-cancer medication. Asked what motivated him to become a research physician, he explained that starting at the age of seven, he accompanied his father, a Rabbi in Columbus, Ohio, on hospital visits to see patients. It was those visits with his father that motivated him to seek a career in medicine.

Children learn best by observing behavior that is modeled by others. While parents are eager to improve their children's behavior in the school setting, it is difficult to provide them with proper role modeling since they are not present at school. *Seven Steps to Mentschhood* is based upon a series of Torah lessons that follow an orderly and intellectually challenging pattern of instruction and guidance that parent and child can discuss together. It fills part of the role modeling void by presenting practical examples of school-based situations through which parents may engage in role-playing activities. As many of these authentic situations are equally applicable to behaviors that occur among siblings at home, they further lend themselves to meaningful, reality-based, parent-child discussions.

Readability

Much of *Seven Steps to Mentschhood* can be read and understood by students of the middle grades. It is recommended that parents and children read selected portions together, particularly those that inspire discussion and child input.

The School/Home Connection

The primary purpose of *Seven Steps to Mentschhood* is to connect the home with the schools' ongoing efforts to help their children treat one another with greater empathy and understanding. As parents review the content of each "step" together with their children, they are encouraged to discuss instances in which the child puts them into action. Liberal praise should be provided by parents to reinforce the behavior and to convey their pleasure and pride as their child adopts and models new behavioral values. Parents should always be on the lookout for these behaviors at home, especially toward and among siblings.

By creating the school/home connection, the goals of *Seven Steps to Mentschhood* are mutually reinforced and are more connected to real life experiences. In this way, children have an enhanced opportunity to internalize them and achieve success.

The Foundation of Mentschhood

Over the past few years there has been much talk about a social movement known as "Random Acts of Kindness." The idea behind this moving and virtuous program is to encourage people to strive toward leaving their personal, mundane existence and give of themselves to others – not out of a sense of obligation but for no reason other than a sense of love.

Seven Steps to Mentschhood

This is most certainly a beautiful concept and, in fact, is very much our goal in teaching children to perform גמילות חסדים, acts of *chessed* (lovingkindness). The problem, however, is the word "random." If we leave the decision to act compassionately toward one another to one's having the urge to do so, there are many who may remain caught up in the challenges of daily life and won't be inspired to help or respond to the needs of his fellow man. *Seven Steps to Mentschhood* seeks to resolve this shortcoming by training children to act kindly, using the solid structure of the Torah as a guide. When the opportunity arises for someone to act altruistically on behalf of others, the Torah shows the way.

We find the well-known reference to תיקון עולם – *tikun olam* (repair of the world) in our עלינו (*Aleinu*) prayer. This phrase is used frequently to refer to man's obligation to make the world a better place. What is usually missing is the rest of this phrase: לתקן עולם במלכות שדי – "to repair the world *through the Almighty's sovereignty*." The way to help fashion a better world is Hashem's Biblical directive. The pathway toward compassionate and *mentschlich* behavior is paved by the mitzvot in the Torah and by our Rabbis, who interpret them for us. This is the foundation of "Mentschhood."

It is hoped that through close interaction with their parents, children will learn to apply the Steps to their everyday interactions with peers both at school and home, and by observing such behavior, the discerning observer will be inspired to declare,

"Now there is a real MENTSCH!"

Introduction for Parents

"Why can't that school teach the kids to behave like a mentsch?"

"Why can't the yeshiva teach *my* child to be a mentsch?"

Have you ever asked one of these questions? Have you ever *felt* like asking any of them?

After over thirty years of working with parents and children in a Yeshiva setting, it has become abundantly clear to me that virtually all parents want their children to be people of fine character. Aren't we, the Jewish people, known as *rachmanim, baishanim* and *gomlei chassadim* (merciful, humble and kind)?

Yet it is ironic that in recent years, as parents have become increasingly concerned about the character traits of their children, it appears as if those concerns have become more noticeably valid. For no matter how we try to protect and insulate our children, they seem ever more susceptible to the influences of a society that grows more coarse and insensitive each day. The insidious encroachment of the internet and other forms of mass communication and media exposes our children to a culture that actually celebrates the dissolution of ethical and introspective behavior.

As our children's behavior is perceived as being less tolerant and less understanding of one another, parents have turned to the schools and *yeshivot* and demanded that more be done to refine our children's characters. The yeshivot have responded with a variety of traditional and innovative responses to this challenge. Many have had some degree of success, yet all appear to be insufficient to the task.

There are three basic reasons for the limited success of many formal midot (Jewish values) programs. In the first place, most people would agree that for children to learn proper behavior they must be exposed to proper role models. Children will learn how best to improve behavior when they are taught by example, especially peer example. Formal programs appeal to the students' intellect, but – as they are usually initiated and taught by adults – provide limited opportunities for peer modeling.

Secondly, the school sees itself as a partner with the home in forming a child's character. The school is not so much the *definer* of proper character traits as it is a *refiner* of those traits learned in the home, traits that both the family and the school hold in esteem. As such, the school alone cannot be held responsible and accountable for character development.

Third, from the standpoint of engendering pedagogically sound behavioral change, most formal midot programs are likely to be ineffective because they are often based upon memorization, rote learning and paper-and-pencil testing. In fact, they often add much to the source of our current frustration because, on the one hand, the school says, "Look, we have a midot program," while on the other hand, the parents respond by saying, "Then why don't the children behave nicely?"

It is important to understand that such programs usually depend upon *extrinsic* motivation. This means that the students learn to respond with the answers (or behavior) that they know the teacher wants to see. A more effective approach is based upon the development of *intrinsic* motivation in which the child's actions are based upon the values he has already internalized. Simply put, ineffective programs are those that tend to manipulate behavior. More effective approaches to midot development must bring about a change of behavior from within. The child does not do the right thing because he wants to please someone; he learns to do the right thing because it is *right*.

A child who seeks his teacher's approval by sharing his snack with a classmate who left his at home, may be on the right track. However, the child who shares his snack because he doesn't want his classmate to go hungry has clearly internalized a cherished value.

Teaching children to reflect upon ethical principles is a challenging and time-consuming task. But the reward for raising a child who will be described as a "mentsch" is immeasurable.

How to Use This Book

Seven Steps To Mentschhood is designed to promote and enhance co-operation between home and school in their joint efforts at fostering proper Jewish behavior among their elementary age children in and outside of the school setting.

The Steps progress from one to the next in a logical and systematic fashion. It will be most effective if the book is read by parents chapter by chapter followed by a discussion of the content of each chapter with their children. Once the chapter content has been discussed and understood, the focus shifts to discussion about the many real-life situations included in each chapter. These are mostly taken directly from student feedback in the school setting. Parents should encourage their children to discuss the challenges they and their peers face in relating positively with one another, and applaud their efforts at putting the Steps into action. It would be helpful for parents to engage their children in role play.

By becoming sensitive to one another's feelings, and through understanding the significant and powerful role the Torah plays in shaping proper behavior, students will be well on their way to "*mentschhood.*"

A Few Tips for Parents

M inimize your personal reaction when your child complains of mistreatment by peers. Listen attentively and sympathetically; then begin brainstorming coping strategies.

E ncourage your child verbally rather than resorting to reward and punishment.

N ote even minor improvements in your child's personal conduct and express your appreciation for them.

T one down. When discussing difficult circumstances, try to use a soft, unhurried voice. Avoid speaking to children when you are angry or when your child is angry.

S upport your child's efforts at becoming independent. Slowly get used to the fact that it's *his* or *her* life. Treat setbacks as milestones on the road to success.

C onsistently follow your routines, rules and guidelines.

H illel was perhaps the most patient of all men. Was he as patient as an eight-year-old as he was when he was fifty? Be patient with your child and give him time to grow.

Introduction for Students

"Why don't you act like a *mentsch*?"

Have you ever heard your parents, *rebbe* or teacher, or even a perfect stranger ask you this question? How do you feel when you hear it? Do you feel hurt because someone important to you doesn't feel that you know how to act nicely? Do you feel angry that you are misunderstood? Do you feel confused because there are times when you are not really sure what adults want from you? Do you feel frustrated because there are times when grown-ups just don't understand?

Like almost all Yeshiva students, you no doubt want to please your parents, *rebbeim* and teachers. You want everyone to think of you and see you as a mentsch.

There are several reasons why it is so difficult to always act like a mentsch. Here are a few:

(1) **It's not "cool."** It is sometimes extremely difficult to do the right thing when you know that some of your peers will think of you as a "goody-goody." Although there is no easy solution to this problem, it *can* be overcome.

Do you remember what it was like to learn to ride your bicycle? You probably can't forget the falls and the bumps and bruises. Two things enabled you to succeed. One was your determination. Secondly, you learned that with enough practice you could master this or almost any reasonable task.

Seven Steps to Mentschhood provides you with a series of orderly Steps to help you learn how to treat others with understanding and respect. If you ignore the discomforts and are *determined* to learn how to be a fine human being by practicing the guidelines the Torah provides for you, then acting like a mentsch can be as natural to you as riding your bike.

(2) **Sometimes other kids are obnoxious**. We know that Hashem creates us all with the potential to be good people. Sometimes it's a wonder to us how some kids go out of their way to be so difficult. Some kids can be mean, rude, obnoxious, difficult to get along with

and sometimes even appear to *ask* for trouble. Once again, there is no easy answer to this problem.

Perhaps one way of dealing with these situations is to understand that there are children who really don't understand how difficult they happen to be. They are "clueless" about how their behavior is affecting the people around them. *Seven Steps to Mentschhood* gives you a series of guidelines to help you look *past* the other person's behavior and focus on your own. It may be hard to believe but you can actually feel better about *yourself* when you learn how to cope successfully with difficult people, and even learn to help them in the process.

(3) **I don't know what to do**. Sometimes someone tells you to act like a mentsch and you kind of stand there saying to yourself, "What does he *want* from me?" You are really not sure what a mentsch should do in this situation.

Seven Steps to Mentschhood is full of practical advice regarding situations that occur every day in Yeshiva and in schools everywhere. In fact, much of the advice given and many of the suggestions made come from students just like you. By following the Torah's guidelines and the advice of your peers, it will become much easier for you to – ACT LIKE A MENTSCH!

How to Use This Book

As you can tell from the title, this book was designed for your parents to help you learn to be a more successful mentsch, particularly at school. However, that doesn't mean that they do all the work! Many of you can read and understand each of the chapters in this book. The problem with *just* reading this or any book of advice is that we tend to quickly forget its contents.

This book is therefore intended for your parents to discuss each Step with you and to review the advice it contains along with its practical suggestions. As you learn to put these suggestions into practice it will be important and helpful for you to review your efforts with your parents. Although it would also be helpful for you to memorize the Seven Steps, there are no worksheets or tests in this book. All you will need for success is the encouragement of your parents and your personal desire to succeed.

User's Guide

After you have carefully read this book, you will become skilled at explaining the Seven Steps to Mentschhood and understanding how to apply them to real life situations. Nevertheless, even when we learn something at home or at school very well, if we do not continue to review it, it starts to fade from our memory.

In order to derive the most benefit from this program, it is important to follow these steps:

(1) Parents read the chapter.

(2) Where possible, the child reads the chapter.

(3) Parents and child discuss the meaning of the Step discussed in the chapter.

(4) Memorize the *pasuk* or at least the words of the Step.

(5) Parents and child discuss the practical applications of the Step.

(6) Parents offer praise and encouragement for the child's efforts.

(7) Parents look for opportunities to praise the child when the Steps are applied to friends and siblings.

Step ·1·

ואהבת לרעך כמוך

You shall love your fellow man as yourself

לא תקם ולא תטור את בני עמך, ואהבת לרעך
כמוך, אני ה'

You shall not take revenge or bear a grudge against
the members of your people; You shall love your fellow
man as yourself – I am Hashem.   (Vayikra 19:18)

"A good Jew is a caring human being."
—Rabbi Berel Wein

Step #1

What We Learn from Our Rabbis

The Talmud (Shabbat, 31a) tells us of the gentile who approached the great sage, Rabbi Hillel, and demanded that he tell him the content of the Torah while standing on one foot. Hillel answered with these words:

דעלך סני לחברך לא תעביד

That which is hateful to you, do not do to your neighbor.

This fundamental concept is derived from our *pasuk* "love your fellow man as yourself." In the words of Rabbi Akiva, "*Zeh klal gadol ba Torah*" (This is, in fact, the great rule of the Torah). The *Sefer HaChinuch* explains Rabbi Akiva's reasoning: If someone truly loves his fellow man, then he will find it impossible to steal from him or be jealous of him or do anything to hurt him or his property. By following this essential mitzvah we can bring true peace among the people of Israel.

How is it possible for an ordinary person to love someone as himself?

The *Ramban* teaches us that it is almost impossible for an ordinary person to reach such an elevated spiritual level. He explains, therefore, that we may practice this mitzvah by expressing our desire that others have the same rewards and success as we have. *Sforno* explains further that what we should want for our friends is what we would desire if we were in their shoes.

Referring to the word *kamocha* (oneself), the Alter of Slobodka, Rabbi Nosson Zvi Finkel says that just as a person loves himself without requiring any rationale, so one should love others without having to search for reasons.* The *Ba'al Shem Tov* explains still further, as

---

* Based on quoted material from "Realistic Love," an article by Uri Miller in *Kol Torah*, student publication of the Torah Academy of Bergen County (April 1996, Vol. 5, p. 2).

quoted in *Jewish Literacy* by Rabbi Joseph Telushkin*: "Just as we love ourselves despite the faults we know we have, so should we love our neighbors despite the faults we see in them."

Finally, we note that the *pasuk* ends with the words "*ani Hashem*" (for I am Hashem) to teach us that we love others because they are born in the image of Hashem – with a *tzelem Elokim*."

We can understand how avoiding hurtful behavior or wishing others well permits us to follow this mitzvah of **Step #1**. Yet one might wonder, is this really the *full* intent of the mitzvah? Rabbi Yeruchem Levovitz, a student of Rabbi Finkel, answers that it is also necessary to show our love for friends and neighbors by doing constructive things for them.** We can and must show our love with concrete and supportive actions.

A Story from Our Past

Long ago there were two brothers who inherited a field from their father, which they divided equally. One of the brothers had a large family while the other was childless.

When it came time for the harvest, the brother with the family said to himself, "My brother is sad because he has no family. Perhaps I can make him feel happier by giving him more grain." So late that night, he took several sheaves of grain and placed them in his brother's storehouse.

At the very same time, the childless brother said to himself, "My brother has a large family and needs the grain more than my wife and I do." So late that night, he took several sheaves of grain and placed them in his brother's storehouse.

This went on for quite some time until one night the two brothers happened upon one another on their way to each other's storehouses, and discovered each other's secret. They warmly embraced and swore that their love for one another would never end.

---

* New York: William Morrow & Company, 1991, p. 63.
** Paraphrased from "Realistic Love" (Miller, *Kol Torah*).

When Hashem looked down upon this touching scene He said, "Here on this spot where two brothers demonstrated such love, one for the other, the *Beit Hamikdash* shall be built."

A Story of the Present***

A woman went into a convenience store to buy a few items, which totaled $4.80. She handed the cashier a twenty-dollar bill and waited for her change. At that point, the store manager angrily called the cashier to the back of the store. When she returned she handed the customer twenty cents. The customer protested and said that she owes her $15.20 because she had paid with a twenty-dollar bill. The cashier adamantly denied this and said that she had only given her a five-dollar bill.

This went on for some time until the customer asked for her receipt and a pen and said, "Here is my name and phone number. When you count up the money in the cash register tonight you will see that you are fifteen dollars over. If you need the money for yourself, please take it as a gift from me. If not, give me a call."

Later that night, the woman received a call form the cashier who apologized profusely and asked for her address so that she could bring the money to her that night. The lady told her to hold on to the money and that she would stop by in the morning to pick it up. When the woman arrived at the store, the embarrassed cashier began to apologize again. The customer responded, "No one needs to be sorry, we should be celebrating; because yesterday, both of us met at least one honest person."

Lessons from the Stories

The story of the two brothers is one of the most enduring and beautiful stories in all of Jewish history. It seems to touch the hearts of all who recognize the purity of the love and devotion the brothers had for one another. For many, this story represents the most ideal

---

*** Based on original article from the syndicated "Ask Ann Landers" column, as seen in *the Record* of Hackensack, NJ, October 7, 1995, p. SL-2.

expression of **Step #1** – "Love your fellow man as yourself." It also demonstrates that the appropriate form of practicing this mitzvah is by actively doing something tangible for the other person.

The story of the woman in the convenience store teaches us many lessons. One might imagine that most people would become enraged by the cashier's behavior and either demand the money or to see the manager. After all, we already have an idea that the manager was not in a good mood, perhaps because of something else the cashier had done to displease him.

However, this customer realized that the cashier might have been rattled by the summons to the manager and didn't want to further agitate her. She made an assumption that under normal circumstances the cashier was an honest person, which turned out to be true. She also refused to let the cashier take the time to rush over to her home to repay the money. Most of all, she saved the cashier much embarrassment by paying her a compliment by telling her that she knew she was honest.

There can be no doubt that the customer treated the cashier the way she, herself, would like to be treated under similar circumstances.

Learning to Apply Step #1 in School

ואהבת לרעך כמוך – Love your fellow man as yourself – is the most logical choice for **Step #1** in acquiring Mentschhood. It is fundamentally important in guiding us in the proper way to treat one another in our many daily interactions.

However, it is not always so easy to "love" the other person or do nice things for him especially when there are feelings of anger or tension that get in the way. Although it is not part of **Step #1**, the first part of our pasuk is very helpful in teaching us how to apply this Step in school.

The pasuk is introduced with the commandment, לא תקם ולא תטר את בני עמך (You shall not take revenge and you shall not bear a grudge against the members of your people).

The best way to understand these two concepts – revenge and bearing a grudge – is with the following example:

You are about to go on a trip and you realize that your camera is broken. You run to your next-door neighbor and ask to borrow his camera. Without any explanation, he says, "No."

Several months later the same thing happens to your neighbor – his camera is broken right before leaving on a trip and he asks you if he may borrow your camera. You have three basic ways of responding:

(1) "No, you may not borrow my camera because you didn't let me borrow yours." This would be called taking **revenge**.

(2) "Yes, you can borrow my camera because I won't be selfish like you were to me when I asked to borrow yours." This would be called bearing a grudge.

(3) "Certainly you may borrow my camera. Enjoy your trip!" This would be the proper way to follow **Step #1** because you would be treating your neighbor as you would like to be treated, not as your neighbor happened to treat you.

If you are able to follow this course of behavior shown in example #3, three things are likely to happen:

(1) You will feel really good about yourself.

(2) Your friends will learn to do the right thing by your example.

(3) You will contribute to a greater sense of peace and harmony.

The following actual conversation took place between two fourth-grade girls:

Shani: "Rachel, I heard you say that you would help Jenny with her homework."

Rachel: "Yes I did."

Shani: "But even after she hurt your feelings and made fun of you?"

Rachel: "Yes, of course I'm going to help her – she's a person who needs help, and it doesn't matter if we're friends or not."

It is very difficult to act as Rachel did. This is the challenge of learning to apply **Step #1** in school.

Everyday Examples in School

The following list was compiled by Yeshiva students to demonstrate some of the many ways we can perform the mitzvah of "Love your fellow man as yourself" in school. Naturally this list does not cover all of the endless possible situations and opportunities.

- If someone loses something, help him find it.

- If someone drops something, help him pick it up.

- If someone is sick, take him to the nurse.

- If you see a fight break out, try to break it up.

- Try not to embarrass someone who does something foolish.

- Avoid making noise in the hallways, because it disturbs other classes.

- If someone feels left out, invite him to join you.

- If someone is carrying something heavy, offer to help.

- Help the person who is putting away the *seforim*.

- If someone is late, help him catch up.

- If someone forgot his supplies, share yours with him.

- Don't interrupt someone who is talking.

- Compliment someone who is wearing something new or nice.

- Compliment someone who is doing something nice.

- Don't laugh at or tease anyone.

- Don't leave people out when playing a game.

- If you hear someone speaking *lashon hara*, help him stop.

- If your team wins, say something nice to the losing team.

- Help new students feel comfortable.

- Help a child who can't find his bus at dismissal time.

- If someone tries something difficult for him and he fails, say, "Good try!"

- If you borrow something from someone, be sure to return it on time.

- Be encouraging to classmates who say, "I'm just stupid!"

- If someone is having difficulty with his school work, help him.

- Don't be bossy.

- Don't cheat.

- Don't tease.

- Don't show off.

- Don't act like a wise-guy.

- Try to help someone before he gets into trouble.

- If there are no more chairs, share yours with someone.

- Don't go through someone's property.

- Keep your promises.

- Help younger children in the hallway or on the playground.

- If someone doesn't know the answer to the teacher's question, give that person time before raising your hand.

- Help someone understand why people are laughing at him.

- Try to avoid telling secrets.

- Congratulate fellow students when they do something special.

- Avoid calling out.

- Help visitors find their way around the school.

- If someone gets out of control in class, help him calm down.

- Volunteer to sit near someone no one else wants to sit near.

- Volunteer to be a partner with someone that no one else wants to work with.

- Help others to solve problems without using hands or fists.

- Try not to let your friend[s] down.

Over the next few weeks, it would be very helpful to have your child tell you about all the times he or she was able to perform this mitzvah while interacting with classmates and under what specific circumstances. Perhaps you might discuss this at your Shabbat table. In order to help him or her keep focused and remember the details of each example, it is also suggested that your child keep a daily record of these events in a loose-leaf binder or notebook.

Parents, please share the following two sections with your child.

For the Student: How to Perform Step #1 in School

Now that you understand **Step #1** and how often we have an opportunity to perform its important principles – especially in the classroom – the following guidelines will help you put them into action:

(1) Think about *choices*. Each and every day we are faced with numerous choices in our lives. There are the easier ones, like what to wear in the morning, or what to have for breakfast; and there are more difficult ones, like whether to stick up for an unpopular classmate or ignore the obnoxious behavior of a younger brother. You are in charge of yourself, and you are the ONLY person who can make your choices for you.

(2) Think about *right & wrong*. By now, most children your age usually know when something is right or wrong. However, sometimes the right thing to do may be the much more difficult choice to make. **Step #1** now provides you with the solution. When facing that difficult choice, ask yourself, "How would I want to be treated in this situation?" If you answer honestly, you will almost always make the right decision.

(3) Parents are *partners* in decision making. Although you must make the final decisions regarding how you treat others, your parents are eager to help you learn to choose the proper path. But remember: Do *not* ask them to tell you what to do. As you review the choices you have in each situation, share them and let your parents *guide* you toward the best decision.

For the Student: What Would *You* Do?

(1) One exciting evening in the fall of 1996, a twelve-year-old boy named Jerry* was sitting in the right-field bleachers of Yankee Stadium. It was the second game of the American League playoff series between the New York Yankees and the Baltimore Orioles.

The home-team shortstop was at the plate and suddenly a powerful line drive was zooming straight toward Jerry. Instead of waiting for the ball to clear the fence, the exuberant Jerry reached over, and the ball caromed off his glove and into the stands. The umpire, not having seen what Jerry had done, declared it a home run. The Oriole outfielder was enraged because he felt that without the boy's interference he might have caught the ball. Nevertheless, the umpire's call was final.

That night, and over the next few days, Jerry was treated like a hero. He was mobbed by reporters wherever he went and was invited to several network television shows. He became the most popular student at his school. Naturally, the fans in Baltimore didn't exactly feel the same way about Jerry's behavior. The game, which the Yankees won by a score of 5–4 in eleven innings, might have ended differently were it not for his interference.

A great debate arose over whether or not Jerry was a true hero. Many New Yorkers felt that he most certainly was, while Baltimore fans felt equally strong about the fact that he was not only not heroic, but also was guilty of disturbing the legitimate play of the game. **Would you treat Jerry like a hero?**

The best solution to this debate could have easily been determined by anyone familiar with **Step #1** and asking a simple question: How would the Yankee fans have reacted if the situation were reversed and the same thing had happened with the Orioles at bat back home in Baltimore? It becomes clear that there can be no doubt that Jerry's actions were not heroic.** They certainly weren't to the Oriole fans. Just as clearly, any honest Yankee fan would admit that Jerry

---

* Not his real name.

** We should also be clear about the meaning of the word "hero." Often, people refer to sports figures as heroes when they probably mean something else. Someone is a hero when he deliberately places himself in danger on behalf of someone else.

wouldn't be considered a hero if the tables were turned. By following the Sforno's advice and putting ourselves "in one another's shoes," we could easily recognize that his behavior was not just *un*heroic, but was actually hurtful to many. This episode helps us better understand Hillel's words: "That which is hateful to you, do not do to your neighbor."

(2) One of the greatest men of the last century, if not our entire history, was the sainted Rabbi Yisrael Meir Kagan, better known as the Chafetz Chaim. His pen name, Chafetz Chaim, is the title of his masterwork on loshon hara, literally "evil tongue," which addresses the prohibition of speaking slander, tale-bearing and gossip.

When the great Rabbi Yisrael Meir Kagan, the Chafetz Chaim, was a young boy, he lived in a small, poor town in Poland. One of the necessary jobs in the town was that of the water carrier. During the cold weather, young boys his age would play a trick on the water carrier and fill his pail with water so that it would freeze overnight. When the carrier awoke in the morning he would be forced to chop the ice out of the pail so that he could do his job.*

What would you do?

Many might suggest that Yisrael Meir simply tell the boys to stop. But he knew that they probably wouldn't listen to him. So he would get up in the middle of the night and empty the pails so that the water carrier would not have to start his day in such an unpleasant fashion.

Related Quotes from Pirkei Avot

{
יהי כבוד חברך חביב עליך כשלך.
"Let the honor of your fellow man be as dear to you as your own." (2:15)
}

When we see honor bestowed upon someone, it is hard for us not to feel that we should be honored as well. A person should therefore

---

* Story paraphrased with permission, from *Love Your Neighbor* by Zelig Pliskin (Union City, NJ: Gross Bros. Printing, 1977, p. 308).

treat others with the honor that he, himself would wish to have, were he in the same situation.

ואל תדין את חברך עד שתגיע למקומו.
and do not judge your fellow man until you have reached his place. (2:5)

You never know what pressures and difficulties might beset another person. You never know how *you* might react under those same conditions. Therefore, treat other people as you would wish to be treated under similar circumstances.

■ □ ■

If you have a story or personal success in performing the step of loving your fellow man as yourself, please share it by sending it to sevensteps@mentschhood.com and putting "Step #1" in the subject line.

Step ·2·

לא תשנא את אחיך בלבבך

You shall not hate your brother in your heart

לא תשנא את אחיך בלבבך, הוכח תוכיח את עמיתך ולא תשא עליו חטא.

You shall not hate your brother in your heart; you shall correct your fellow man and not bear a sin because of him. *(Vayikra 19:17)*

Mentschlichkeit: The quality of being "a kind, caring, sensitive person who thinks of others besides himself."
—Rabbi Pesach Krohn

Step #2

Now that we know we are supposed to treat one another with love, let us learn what to do about those people who are so very difficult to love because they behave in ways that are improper or even hurtful to both the individual and the community. They are, in fact, people about whom we might say: "I hate that person!"

What We Learn from Our Rabbis

Why does the Torah admonish us so strongly to refrain from hating someone in our hearts? More specifically, why, if no one even knows, must we eliminate hatred that is inside our hearts and known only to ourselves? The *Yad Haketanah* provides an important insight. When someone has hatred bottled up inside of himself, without acknowledging it or expressing it, it is like an internal fire that is not extinguishable. However, once a person is able to express himself by sharing his feelings, this burning hatred is released.

The release of hatred, however, must be carried out very carefully. While we are commanded to eliminate hatred from our hearts and let someone know when he has done something wrong to us, Hashem also tells us how this rebuke must be carried out. The key to this process is connected to **Step #1**: to remember to treat one another *b'ahava* – with love. In Talmud *Yoma* (9b), we learn that the second *Beit Hamikdash* was destroyed because of *sinat chinom*, needless hatred of one another. Yet in Talmud *Shabbat* (119b) we learn that it was destroyed because the people failed to rebuke or correct one another's wrongdoings. Why does the Gemara suggest two different reasons?

The answer, says the *Mayana Shel Torah*, is that harboring needless hatred in one's heart and failing to rebuke our brethren both reflect an absence of love. The more we truly care for our neighbors, the more successful and effective will be the correction.

The *Mayana* continues that this is the reason the pasuk uses the term *amitecha* – your friend. One should not only be interested in simply telling someone he has sinned, but one must also have a desire to help him improve. Therefore we are taught that we chastise or correct someone by raising his self-esteem and not by lowering it.

The *Sefat Emet* expands on this idea by suggesting that when people sin, we might consider it a collective failing on our part because we haven't done enough for the sinner to prevent his misbehavior. Had we been more vigilant, the sinner might have repented and mended his ways. In fact, the *Ramban* says that by failing to rebuke people who have acted sinfully, we may bear some of the guilt of his future transgressions. This explains the words ולא תשא עליו חטא – that we must not bear a sin because of him.

We also learn from this the importance of not embarrassing someone when giving rebuke. The *Rambam* teaches us that a person who embarrasses his friend in public forfeits the world to come. When correcting a person's behavior we must do it in a soft voice, indicating that our efforts are for his best interest. If the person rejects the rebuke, we must continue to offer it until he agrees to change.

Rabbi Eliyahu Dessler expands upon this concept with his meaningful insight: A person's rebuke must come from the depths of one's heart because only then will it find its way into the sinner's heart. This level of commitment is continuously reinforced as we strive to always to keep in mind that we are all created *b'tzelem Elokim* – in Hashem's image. Finally, our rabbis instruct us to approach the task of correcting others with an appropriate degree of humility. This follows their penetrating admonition, *"Kishot et atzmecha v'achar kach kishot acherim"* – Improve yourself before improving others.

A Related Mitzvah

In Parshat Mishpatim we learn:

> כי תראה חמור שנאך רבץ תחת משאו וחדלת מעזוב לו, עזוב
> תעזוב עמו
> If you see the donkey of someone you hate crouching under its burden, would you stop from helping him; You shall surely help him.

Rashi explains that this is actually a question: Will you stop from helping him? You can relate this mitzvah to our "step" as follows: If you had been friendly with someone whom you had helped in the past, now that you hate him for something he has done, would you stop from helping him? No, the Torah says, even though he may have wronged you, it is your responsibility to help him.

Another question is asked: Why does it say *"imo,"* *along* with him rather than just "help him"? Rabbi Yissachar Frand explains that even if we hate the person, we must overcome our natural inclination not to help him, because by doing the right thing, it is actually an excellent way to repair the friendship.

A Story from Our Past

In chapter one, you read the touching story of the two brothers who were so devoted to each other. It was on the basis of their mutual love that Hashem declared that the Beit Hamikdash would be built upon their land. The story that follows sadly represents the very opposite. It is the story of Kamtza and Bar Kamtza.

Before the destruction of the Second Beit Hamikdash, a man held a feast and invited all his friends including Kamtza. He also had an enemy named Bar Kamtza and, as luck would have it, the messenger delivered the invitation to Bar Kamtza instead of Kamtza.

Bar Kamtza arrived at the party pleased because he assumed that the host invited him so that they could once again be friends. However, when the host saw him, he tried to have him thrown out. Bar Kamtza immediately realized that a mistake had been made, and in order to avoid being publicly embarrassed, offered to pay for his own meal. The host remained adamant so Bar Kamtza offered to pay for half the other meals and then finally the entire feast, but the host would not relent and threw him out.

Angry and humiliated, Bar Kamtza ran to the Roman authorities claiming that the Jews were rebelling. The Romans were happy to concur with his charges, and this eventually led to the loss of Yerushalayim and the Second Beit Hamikdash.

A Story of Recent Times

Paraphrased from the *New York Times*, December 27, 1998.

Several years ago, in 1950, a young, Jewish girl about ten years of age was sitting in her classroom in a school in Switzerland. Her stern teacher would often make disparaging comments about Jews. It was not long after the Holocaust had taken place, and although Switzerland declared itself neutral during the war, it was not a friendly country toward Jews.

The young girl, worried about calling attention to herself, yet wanting to change her teacher's attitudes, started to think about what she might do.

She went home and, that night, wrote about the long history of Jewish persecution in great detail. When she was finished, she brought it to her teacher and said, "I am weak in spelling, could you correct this?"

Lessons from the Stories

Story #1: A question is asked regarding the story of Kamtza and Bar Kamtza. How is it possible that all of the Jewish people were punished because of one person? As Bar Kamtza was leaving the feast suffering terrible embarrassment, there were several sages present, yet not one person stood up for him. Every one of them failed to live up to the directive of **Step #2** – to correct the person who sins. Such callousness was symbolic of the behavior of the general population who were thereby judged not worthy of having the Beit Hamikdash in their midst.

Story #2: Although her teacher was not a Jew, the young girl was still faced with the challenge of correcting him without making things even worse for herself. Her very clever plan was the perfect solution. It is interesting to note that years later, in 1998, this brave young lady became the first Jewish female president of Switzerland.

A Recurring Story

Rabbi Naftali Reich explains that constructive criticism delivered in the spirit of love and compassion can be a catalyst for positive personal growth. He tells the following story* to explain:

In a certain district of Jerusalem, all the storekeepers agreed to close down their stores for Shabbos – except for one grocer. No matter how much pressure was brought upon him, he refused to budge.

One Friday, one of the prominent Jerusalem sages, dressed in his best Shabbos finery, entered the grocery store. He stationed himself on a chair in the back of the store and proceeded to stay there for the entire day, watching the busy hustle and bustle of the grocery shoppers. As evening drew near, the grocer approached the sage and asked, "Is everything alright, rabbi? Do you need anything? Is there anything I can do to help you?" "No," said the sage. "I have come because I wanted to understand why you refused to close your store on Shabbos. Now, it is clear to me. You have such a busy store that it would be a tremendous ordeal for you to close it, even for one day."

The grocer burst into tears. "You are the first one to try to see it from my side," he managed to say between sobs. "Everyone scolded and berated me, but before you, no one tried to understand me."

After that day, it was not long before the grocer agreed to close his store on Shabbos. A few kind words had been effective where threats and invective had failed.

A Story for All Time

A few years ago, Rabbi Sholmo Riskin, Chief Rabbi of Efrat, Israel was delivering a lecture on Rabbi Kagan, the Chafetz Chaim, and he told this story:

There was a young man in the Chafetz Chaim's Yeshiva in the town of Radin in Poland during the early part of the 20th century. This student was caught smoking on Shabbat. Such behavior was considered quite scandalous and was grounds for expulsion. Before he was asked to leave, the Chafetz Chaim asked to speak with the boy. As

---

* Text copyright 2008 by Rabbi Naftali Reich and www.Torah.org.

the story was told, in two minutes he had convinced the young man to change his ways.

Rabbi Riskin said that he would give anything to know what it was that the Chafetz Chaim had said that would have that kind of impact. While he was talking, he noticed that there was an old man in his audience who began to tremble uncontrollably. At the conclusion of the lecture the man approached him and said, "I'm that man! It happened to me!" The man then told his story:

"It was in the late 1920s. I was very young and the Chafetz Chaim was in his eighties. He was very short and barely came up to my shoulder. I was in the Chafetz Chaim's private residence and I noticed that there wasn't a single piece of furniture that was not broken. He came up to me, grabbed on to my arm tightly and out of his mouth came the word, 'Shabbos,' said with so much feeling it was as if it were the most precious thing in the world.

"Then there was silence. Soon he began to cry streams of tears that trickled down the palm of my hand. I couldn't forget how hot those tears felt. Then I heard one more word, 'Shabbos,' said with an overwhelming sense of love and joy, and with that, he escorted me to the door."

Rabbi Riskin said, "When I heard the story I couldn't stop shuddering. I could almost imagine those tears on my hand, and what the word 'Shabbos' must have sounded like, uttered in that room in Radin, decades ago."

Appreciating the Story

It would have been so easy to expel the young man from the Yeshiva, and get rid of this awful person who might have a negative impact upon the other students. This is, in fact, what often happens these days in many yeshivot. But the Chafetz Chaim could not bear to lose this young man to his faith and *yiddishkeit,* and he felt compelled to try to rescue him. The rest of the story was predictable, as the young man, whose faith was renewed, grew to enjoy an observant lifestyle and beautiful family.

What is so remarkable is the application of this story to **Step #2.** When correcting the sinner, we are warned to be careful to do it without causing a sin. The Chafetz Chaim achieved this goal by uttering a single word two times.

Embarrassment

Mishna 15 in *Perek Gimel* of *Avot* warns us about embarrassing or humiliating someone in front of others. One of the common elements in the stories you've just read is the great lengths that righteous people will go to, to avoid embarrassing someone. Why is this so important? The actual words of this mishna are quite instructive and provide our answer: והמלבין פני חברו ברבים ("one who humiliates his fellow in public"). The word מלבין actually means "to whiten" and is used as a metaphor for embarrassment. Our Rabbis teach us that embarrassing someone is compared to shedding someone's blood because the sensation of humiliation will actually cause the blood to drain from the victim's face. Everyone at one time or another has experienced this trauma, and each of us should do whatever we can to avoid inflicting this pain on others.

Learning to Apply Step #2 in School

As we learn from our Rabbis, correcting people's misbehavior is a very challenging task. Not only is it uncomfortable to rebuke a fellow student's wrongdoing, it is also very difficult because we want our efforts to result in a positive change and not create an even worse situation. Fortunately, there are several strategies one may use to help students achieve their goal. Among them:

(1) The "I" Message

Original idea from Dr. Thomas Gordon's *PET – Parent Effectiveness Training: The Tested New Way To Raise Responsible Children* (New York, NY: Peter H. Wyden Inc., 1970, p. 115).

When someone does something to you that is upsetting, and particularly if it occurs often, it usually doesn't help to get angry at the person and demand that he stop. It also doesn't help to lecture him about what he has done to upset you. In fact there are often times that some people deliberately try to be annoying or upsetting. At these times it is helpful to consider using an "I" message. "I" messages are a way of stating how you feel without attacking the other person. There is a very simple format for delivering the "I" message:

(1) Use the person's name

(2) Tell how you feel

(3) Tell why

(4) Tell what you want

For example:

(1) Shlomo

(2) I feel angry

(3) when you push me on line.

(4) Please stop it.

Or:

(1) Shani

(2) I feel embarrassed

(3) every time you whisper things about me behind my back.

(4) Please be a better friend and stop.

Please note:

(1) It is very important to remember that the offender may not stop after receiving an "I" message. It may take several messages, but eventually he will get tired of trying to upset you and will stop. If not, it might be necessary to ask an adult at school for help.

(2) When delivering an "I" message, always do it quietly and with no one else nearby. (Try it at recess or snack time.)

(3) "I" messages can help with brothers and sisters as well.

(2) Advice for Delivering Rebukes

When correcting someone who is doing the wrong thing, it will be helpful to keep the following in mind:

(1) Try to imagine what is causing the person to do the wrong thing. This is sometimes referred to as "standing in someone's shoes." If you can understand his reasons it will help you offer advice instead of simply correcting him.

(2) Try to conduct a conversation before offering a rebuke. A willingness to listen might encourage some mutually agreed upon solutions.

(3) Sometimes it might pay to ignore certain behavior and wait until you might have a better opportunity for success.

(4) Always try your best to model the kind of behavior you want others to emulate.

(3) Six Steps in Conflict Resolution

Paraphrased from an article by Albert Low, adapted from *Creating the Peaceable School: Program Guide: A Comprehensive Program for Teaching Conflict Resolution* by Richard Bodine, Donna Crawford, and Fred Schrumpf (Champagne, Illinois: Research Press, p.12).

Since it is inevitable that conflicts will arise in classrooms as they do everywhere else in life, experts in this area recommend the following:

(1) Identify the problem without placing the blame on anyone.

(2) Brainstorm several solutions.

(3) Evaluate each of the solutions with everyone involved.

(4) Decide on the best possible solution.

(5) Work out ways of implementing the solution.

(6) Follow up and determine how well the solution is working.

Everyday Examples in School

The following list was compiled by Yeshiva students to demonstrate some of the many ways that students can cause others to hate their behavior in school. They are behaviors about which someone is likely to say, "I hate that person!"

Naturally, this list does not cover all the endless possibilities.

Seven Steps to Mentschhood

- Making fun of someone.
- Making fun of someone's appearance or looks.
- Deliberately hurting someone's feelings.
- Boys and girls making fun of each other.
- Name calling.
- Lecturing people.
- Always calling out things that have nothing to do with the lesson.
- Telling someone who is angry what to do.
- Taking people's belongings without permission.
- Making an unfair call in sports.
- Making fun of someone who isn't good at sports.
- Bragging about how much better you are than the other person or team
- Telling lies.
- Hitting or hurting people.
- Telling secrets about someone in view.
- Pulling someone out of the line.
- Leaving people out of a game.
- Bragging about test marks.
- Borrowing something and not returning it.
- Gossiping and speaking *lashon hara*.
- Making fun of someone's work.
- Someone gets something wrong on the board and another person says, "Oooooh that's soooo easy!"
- Taking revenge.
- Making fun of someone's grades.
- Drawing on someone's work.

- Blaming someone else for something wrong you did.

- Making fun of someone's background.

- Not sharing when someone needs something.

- Your partner does all the work and you do none of it.

- Not sticking up for a friend if he is being picked on.

- Throwing food at someone during lunch.

- Saving seats during lunch.

- Copying someone's work without permission.

- Laughing at someone who is clueless.

For the Student: How to Perform Step #2 in School

Over the next few weeks, ask your child to tell you if he or she has seen any of the above behaviors at school. Ask whether your child or a classmate tried to correct the offender and what the outcome was. **It is very important for children to understand that it isn't enough to stay away from people who misbehave. Wherever possible it is everyone's obligation to rebuke people who are hurtful to others.**

It is also important for adults to realize that although some of the items on the list might seem somewhat trivial, each one is very significant to at least some students in any given classroom. Sometimes adults might not recall how sensitive they were as young children.

Parents can also help their children perform this step by engaging them in role play.

Here's an easy way to remember how to perform Step #2: A child should always try to avoid any behavior that might make someone hate her, thereby avoiding the need for rebuke.

> *When asked why the pasuk in* **Step #2** *speaks specifically about the heart, a fourth grader said: "It's because when people treat others badly it's like* **ripping apart someone's heart**.*"*

For the Student: What Would *You* Do?

There is a true story, recounted in *Love Your Neighbor* by Rabbi Zelig Pliskin (p. 280), about a non-religious, Jewish person who inadvertently ended up driving his car through a religious neighborhood in Yerushalayim on Shabbat. He was surprised to find the roadway blocked off by a barrier. This made him furious and he began a weekly practice of driving through religious neighborhoods on Shabbat to upset and antagonize the local residents. On one Shabbat, as he stopped to move a barrier aside, a local resident came up to him and . . .

At this point in the story, I would stop and ask my students what they would say or do if they were the one who approached the man while he was removing the barrier. I added that the answer had to be reflective of **Step #2**: Telling someone that he was doing something wrong and not making things worse while doing it.

Most of the time the students would say things like:

- "This is my Shabbat. Please don't drive through here."

- "It's not nice to upset people on their special day."

- "How would you like it if someone did the same thing to you?"

I would then tell the students that most of their suggestions could be seen by the driver as being lectured to. I said that most people, children and adults alike, do not like to be lectured or talked down to. In fact, some of their suggestions would actually raise another barrier between the man and the driver. Although this barrier was invisible, it could easily make the situation worse.

I then told the students the rest of the story.

The resident stopped him with a smile on his face and asked for the driver's name and address, which he gave him. The driver was quite surprised when, that night, the man paid a visit to his home. For two hours, with much love and deep feeling, the man told him all about the benefits of Torah observance.

In that one evening, the driver's life was changed forever. Learning about his religion and its practices from such a warm and passionate perspective, inspired him to become an observant Jew. Today, all his children attend Yeshiva in Yerushalayim.

What do we learn from the man who stopped the driver? The following are some of the lessons to remember about this story:

- He greeted him with a warm smile.

- He didn't judge him.

- He didn't tell him what to do or not to do.

- He didn't lecture him about his behavior.

- He took the time to teach him in a way that would be heard and accepted.

- He succeeded in making the man a *shomer Shabbat* and *mitzvot* (Torah-observant) Jew.

In short, the man followed **Step #2** in a most practical and successful way. He remembered what our Rabbis have taught us – that when we come across someone doing the wrong thing, we are all in part responsible for his actions, so we must help him learn what he has done wrong, and help correct the behavior so that it will not bring either of them to sin.

Related Quotes from Pirkei Avot

והוי דן את כל האדם לכף זכות

and judge everyone favorably (1:6)

As we go through life we are bound to come across people whose behavior disappoints us. As a consequence, we might tend to judge people harshly. The Mishna teaches us that we must try to suspend those negative thoughts and judge people as if their intentions were good.

This mishna also uses the word **kol ha'adam**, which would normally mean "all of mankind." However, we may interpret this as meaning that we judge a person by the *totality* of his actions, not just one instance in which he might falter.

> ואל תדין את חברך עד שתגיע למקומו
> Do not judge your fellow until you have reached his place (2:5)

Before we judge someone's behavior, we must try to imagine how we would respond if we were standing in his place. This reflects **Step #1**, in which we would hope that we all treat one another as we would like to be treated in similar circumstances.

> אל תרצה את חברך בשעת כעסו
> Do not appease your fellow at the time of his anger (4:23)

We must always remember to permit someone to calm down before we can even engage in conversation with him. How much more so when we must discuss his inappropriate behavior. Before rebuking someone, we must ask ourselves this question: "If I were in this same situation, would I want someone to criticize me at this time?"

> והמלבין פני חברו ברבים . . . אין לא חלק לעולם הבא.
> [One who] humiliates his fellow in public ... has no share in the World to Come. (3:15)

We have reviewed the almost countless ways that students can hurt one another's feelings at school. The Talmud teaches us that embarrassing someone is like killing him.

The word *malbin* comes from the word "white." When someone is humiliated, the blood is actually drawn from his face and he turns white – frequently, before turning bright red. This is why we are taught that this behavior is akin to bloodshed. Because this is such a serious sin, we must all go out of our way to avoid ever hurting anyone's feelings.

חביב אדם שנברא בצלם
Beloved is man, for he was made in Hashem's image
(3:18)

■ □ ■

Step 2: If you have a story or personal success in overcoming hatred for someone else, or letting someone know in the proper way that he or she has done something wrong, please share it by sending it to sevensteps@mentsch-hood.com and writing "Step #2" in the subject line.

Step
·3·

ולפני עור לא תתן מכשל

And you shall not place a stumbling block before the blind

לא תקלל חרש ולפני עור לא תתן מכשל, ויראת
מאלקיך אני ה׳

You shall not curse the deaf, nor put a stumbling block before the blind, but you shall fear your G-d, for I am Hashem.   (Vayikra 19:14)

**"There is no reason you can't be good – and nice."
—Milford Palmer to his son Arnold, champion golfer.**

Step #3

Now that we know how we are supposed to treat one another, and how to deal with a difficult person in a positive way, we will turn our attention to some of the more subtle behaviors the Torah warns us to avoid.

What We Learn from Our Rabbis

There are many lessons that we learn from the negative commandment (מצות לא תעשה), "Do not place a stumbling block before a blind person."

There is the literal understanding that forbids us from being callous or cruel to handicapped people; however, most commentators focus on the Rambam's interpretation, which is that it forbids us from giving bad advice to an unsuspecting person. This is especially true if one would enjoy personal gain through such an act of deceit. The *Sefer Hachinuch* adds that we follow this law in order to bring about a betterment of our world by making sure that people are guided along the proper path.

A person must avoid assuming that if his advice causes damage to another person, then he is not responsible because it was an indirect act. The Sforno teaches us that even if a person is indirectly responsible, by extension, he violates this mitzvah. This scenario is likened to the person who digs a hole in a public place and is responsible for someone who falls in and is injured.

Rabbi Moshe Chaim Luzzato, in *Mesilat Yisharim* (ch. 11), says that it is the duty of an upright person to give the kind of advice that he, himself would follow in the same situation (**Step #1**). If he is fearful of being hurt by offering the advice, he is not permitted to be misleading, but should instead excuse himself and give no advice at all. On this point, the Pele Yoetz says that even if someone could be hurt financially by giving the correct advice, he should do so anyway because "Hashem will doubly repay him."

Another significant element of this mitzvah is to make sure that all the advice that one gives is correct according to *halacha* (Jewish law). To make this point crystal clear, the very next *pasuk* begins with the words, לא תעשו עול במשפט (You shall not be unrighteous in judgment), prompting our Rabbis to warn us, הוו מתונים בדין (be very careful and deliberate when rendering judgments).

What about the person who sees wrongdoing and fails to correct it? The *Midrash Hagadol* on our pasuk teaches us that if someone strengthens the hands of a sinner to do the wrong thing, he is guilty of violating this mitzvah. The person who does nothing in the face of evil can certainly be seen as strengthening the sinner's hand (**Step #2**).

Finally, the Ramban explains why this pasuk specifically speaks about cursing the deaf and tripping the blind. In a very literal sense he explains that when we encounter people with these disabilities, we tend to be less afraid of their reactions if we mistreat them. Therefore the pasuk concludes, "ויראת מאלוקיך" (You shall fear Hashem). Even if we are not fearful of our fellow man, we must remember that Hashem sees all.

When they were introduced to this verse for the first time, a group of fourth graders attempted to explain the references to cursing the deaf or tripping the blind. The following are two of their spontaneous interpretations:

> *"It's bad enough to curse someone if they can hear it, but it's even worse to curse them if they are deaf because they can't even hear it. Also, if you do something to someone who can see it's bad, but it's even worse if they can't see because they don't know what happened. If they knew, they could ask for help."*
> —Yehuda

> *"If you curse the deaf, you're cursing Hashem, for Hashem created them [that way]."*
> —Daphna

Applications

There are many behaviors that are derived from this negative commandment that our Rabbis have forbidden. Most of these prohibitions are designed to prevent someone from inadvertently sinning.

*   We may not offer wine to a *nazir* (Nazirite).
    (*He may forget and break his vow of refraining from drinking wine.*)

*   Parents may not hit their grown son.
    (*He may become enraged and sin by striking back.*)

*   We may not sell lethal weapons to a dangerous person.
    (*If he uses them to hurt someone, the seller will be a partner in the sin.*)

*   We may not lend someone money without witnesses present.
    (*When the time comes to pay back the loan, the borrower may be tempted to deny that he borrowed the money.*)

*   We may not speak *lashon hara*.
    (*Both the speaker and listener sin when they engage in lashon hara.*)

*   We may not offer unkosher food to a Jew who does not keep kosher.
    (*We would be assisting him in committing a sin.*)

*   We may not behave in an arrogant fashion.
    (*This can cause people to dislike us and we may violate "You shall not hate your brother in your heart." [**Step #2**]*)

Some of the above selections paraphrased from Rabbi Zelig Pliskin in *Love Your Neighbor*, pp. 256–257.

A Related Mitzvah

{ לא תונו איש את עמיתו
Each of you shall not aggrieve his fellow (Vayikra 25:17)

This negative commandment is known as אונאת דברים – *painful words* or **verbal deception**. It is related to **Step #3** because it also prohibits us from saying things that will deliberately deceive our fellow man. The following* are some examples of this prohibition:

- We may not take the time of a salesperson in a store if we have no intention of buying anything.
  (*We not only mislead him, we may cause him to lose other customers who are there to make a purchase.*)

- This prohibition should also be applied to children.
  (*Parents should avoid hurting their children's feelings or embarrassing them.*)

- We may not invite someone to our house on Shabbat when we know that he will not be in town that weekend.
  (*The person will feel that he has to reciprocate the invitation.*)

- We may not remind a *ba'al teshuvah* about his past sins.
  (*This may cause him much undeserved anguish.*)

- We may not call anyone derogatory names.
  (*Even if we say it is in jest, it can still hurt someone's feelings.*)

- We may not scare a person or play tricks on him.
  (*The sense of discomfort that results is very real.*)

- We may not engage in misleading advertising.
  (*For example, putting less of the product in a larger box.*)

From lecture by Rabbi Chaim Morgenstern (Aish Audio), citing the halachot of *ona'at devarim*, based on Shulchan Aruch, Choshen Mishpat 228:4–5.

Another Related Mitzvah

לא תלך רכיל בעמיך
You shall not go about as a gossipmonger among your people   (Vayikra 19:16)

This is the mitzvah that forbids us from saying *lashon hara* – to speak badly about people behind their backs, even if the information is true.

---

* Based on an NCSY New England Region sourcebook on Lashon Hara, from Junior Spring Regional March 22–24, 1996, p. 6.

The following is a list* of some of the many excuses that people give for saying *lashon hara* (none of them is valid):

- "I wouldn't mind if someone said that about me."

- "He'll never know about it."

- "We're close friends so he won't mind."

- "I did the same thing myself."

- "I was only joking."

- "Everybody knows it anyway."

- "I'd say it even if he were here."

- "But it's true."

Gossip

One could write volumes about the evils of lashon hara, gossip and all other forms of tale-bearing. (The Chafetz Chaim has already done so.) When discussing the many ways we can be hurtful to one another with our speech, my students enjoyed reading the following poem:

Gossip – The History of a Lie
(Author unknown)

First, someone told it,
  Then the room could not hold it,
So busy tongues rolled it
  Till they got it outside.
Then the crowd came across it,
  They stretched it and tossed it,
And never once lost it,
  Till it grew long and wide.
This lie brought forth others,
  Evil sisters and brothers
And fathers and mothers –
  A terrible crew.

As headlong they hurried,
  The people they flurried,
And troubled and worried,
  As lies always do.
So, evil it boded,
  This monstrous lie goaded,
Till at last it exploded
  In sin and in shame.
But from mud and mire,
  The pieces flew higher
Till they hit the sad liar
  And killed his good name.

A Story from Our Past

This is actually the Jewish people's very first story. It is also the first story of deception. It is the story of *Adam*, *Chava* and the *nachash* (Adam, Eve and the serpent). Hashem tells Adam that he may eat from any tree in the Garden of Eden except for the *etz hadaat* – the tree of knowledge. He shares this information with Chava. The cunning serpent tricks Chava into eating from the tree. She then convinces Adam to do the same. When Hashem challenges them for disobeying Him, Adam blames Chava, who, in turn, blames the snake for deceiving her. As a consequence, all three are punished.

A Story from the Present

A recent Jewish immigrant to the United States, while trying to sell his house, was approached by a successful real estate broker who presented him with an offer that was higher than his asking price. The owner readily agreed and was quickly able to find a new home, which he then purchased. When the time came to finalize the sale of his home, the broker added exorbitant costs that the home owner could not afford. Unable to complete the sale of his home, and having already purchased a new one, the poor man had no choice but to agree to pay the additional expenses which would place him in heavy debt.

When challenged by local Rabbis regarding the *halachic* ramifications of his inappropriate actions, the real estate broker said, "Oh, it's just *shtick* [business shenanigans]."

It turns out that this person had done this to other unsuspecting people several times in the past.

Lessons from the Stories

In the first story, we learn that deception can lead to further sin, and can have disastrous consequences. The serpent, having the blessing of speech, used this gift for an evil purpose. Chava, who opened the door to the deception by exaggerating the truth, made things far worse as she caused Adam to join her in sinning. As a result, the punishments that befell Adam and Chava have been visited upon all their future descendents.

In the second story the real estate dealer tricked the homeowner into accepting his offer, knowing all along that he would eventually take advantage of him. He clearly violated the negative commandment of **Step #3** by deliberately placing a "stumbling block" in the path of the homeowner. The dealer caused much anger in the community regarding his despicable tactics, causing many to feel a sense of outrage against him, in violation of **Step #2**.

Learning to Apply Step #3 in School

One of the most common behaviors one finds among children in the school setting is the tendency to make fun of one another and play tricks on each other. More often than not, the child guilty of this behavior will say, "It's just a joke" or, "I was only kidding." But the truth is, no normal person wants to be made fun of or be the butt of jokes. Nor does anyone want to be tricked or made to feel foolish. The problem becomes more complicated when students who might not engage in this behavior run the risk of falling into disfavor with some of the more "popular" classmates by not joining in the "fun."

The problem is exacerbated by the general culture in which we live that promotes this behavior. Hidden camera programs, entertainment "roasts" and panel shows have for decades inspired generations of children and adults to take advantage of others in the name of fun and entertainment. Today's children must deal with a host of technological opportunities that literally brings the entire world to their fingertips.

Instead of the classroom serving as a nurturing environment for empathic and supportive social interaction, the classroom is often a place of anxiety and discomfort for many children. Some wait in fear for the next time a joke will be played on them or that they will be ridiculed in the presence of their classmates.

Understanding Friendship

When adults speak about the "real world" they are usually referring to the world outside of school. However, for children, the real world is very much centered on their classrooms and playing fields. It is the place where they learn how to get along with one another.

One could make a strong argument that the most important skills that children learn in preschool classes are those related to socializing and developing the ability to relate effectively with classmates and friends. Forging close and long-lasting friendships is a goal that all parents and educators have for their children. This endeavor requires many skills that not all children possess. It is very difficult for most of us – student, child or adult alike – to respond effectively to those who deliberately cause discomfort to their peers in violation of **Step #3**. It should be our goal to provide our children with the guidance that will enable them to counter these behaviors and learn to master the art of friendship.

Acquiring and maintaining friendships is a lifelong, ongoing process. The simplest way to start is to identify those qualities that describe a good friend. I have found the following poem to be helpful in beginning this process:

The A to Z of Friendship
(Author unknown)

A ccepts you as you are
B elieves in *you*
C alls you just to say "hi"
D oesn't give up on you
E nvisions the whole of you
F orgives your mistakes
G ives unconditionally
H elps you
I nvites you over
J ust be with you
K eeps you close at heart
L oves you for who you are
M akes a difference in your life
N ever judges

O ffers support
P icks you up
Q uiets your fears
R aises your spirits
S ays nice things about you and
T ells you the truth when you need
   to hear it
U nderstands you
V alues you
W alks beside you
X -plains things you don't under-
   stand
Y ells when you don't listen
Z aps you back to reality

Each of the items in the poem is worthy of a discussion between parent and child.

The following list was compiled by a group of sixth-grade students following a discussion on the verse from Pirkei Avot (1:6):

{ וקנה לך חבר
acquire yourself a friend

A true friend is someone who . . .

(1) Goes out of his way to help his friend.

(2) You can trust with your biggest secrets and you know they'll never tell anyone.

(3) Likes you for who you are (you can be yourself and they appreciate you).

(4) Is your friend no matter what.

(5) Laughs with you, not at you.

(6) Has fun with you. (They're not using you.)

(7) Stands up for you.

(8) Doesn't pressure you to do things you don't want to do.

(9) Respects your opinion and what you say and feel.

(10) Listens to you even if they aren't really interested in what you're saying.

■   □   ■

Considering the anxieties that are often present among children in the classroom and the challenges of maintaining positive friendships, it becomes more than just an academic exercise for them to learn the lessons of **Step #3**. It is, in fact, important for every child's sound and healthy emotional growth and development. One effective way to accomplish this is by recognizing and analyzing the many forms these negative behaviors take on in the classroom and school environment. By studying these behaviors and becoming familiar with them, children and their parents can discuss strategies that will enable them to cope with them or learn how to avoid them.

The list that follows is a compilation of many negative behaviors compiled with the input of students' suggestions over a period of several years.

Everyday Examples in School

It is recommended that parents and children review and discuss this surprisingly varied and comprehensive list. It will sensitize students to their frequent occurrence in the classroom and enable them to respond effectively and appropriately.

- Giving the wrong directions to a new student

- Laughing at people after giving them the wrong directions

- Copying someone's work (without telling him)

- Giving someone the wrong Hebrew translation

- When someone doesn't know something about religion and they ask a question and you tell them they're stupid

- Telling someone who does not yet know the mitzvot that something is a mitzvah but it really isn't

- Tricking someone into giving the wrong answer

- Telling someone at the beginning of the line that the teacher said to go further, but she really didn't

- Giving the wrong information on purpose because you don't like the group you are in

- Telling someone there's no homework when there really is

- Telling someone the water fountain is broken when it isn't

- Cheating on tests/cheating on tests and blaming others

- Scribbling on the board and telling the teacher it was someone else

- Telling someone he can write in print when you are supposed to write in cursive

- Sending someone the wrong notes when he is out sick

- Speaking lashon hara
- Spreading rumors about someone
- Deliberately getting someone in trouble
- Sticking your foot out
- Tripping someone
- Tripping someone and saying you were stretching
- Pulling someone's chair out from behind him
- Telling someone there's something on his shirt, and when he looks down you plunk him in the nose
- "Fun" fighting – but not really
- Giving someone the wrong answer
- Giving someone the wrong homework
- Someone asks you for your notes and you give him the wrong ones
- Telling someone the test is next week (when it's tomorrow)
- When someone is late and you tell him to go to the wrong place
- Laughing at someone for getting the wrong answer
- Telling someone there's a bug on him when there isn't
- Someone has something you want and you say, "Look over there," and then you take it
- Someone asks for help on the computer and you (deliberately) mess it all up
- Taking someone's belongings and putting it in someone else's desk so that the owner yells at the wrong person
- Blaming someone for something he didn't do
- Breaking something and not admitting it
- Ruining something that someone worked very hard at
- Putting thumb tacks on a chair
- Putting "donkey" or "bunny" ears on someone

Seven Steps to Mentschhood

- Telling someone there's an early (snow) dismissal when there isn't
- Teasing
- "Dissing" people
- Speaking sarcastically
- Eavesdropping
- Showing off
- Telling someone you will sit next to him and you sit somewhere else
- Inviting someone to sit next to you in the lunchroom when you know that food is on the chair
- Spoiling someone's food
- Flicking food at someone so he'll respond and get caught
- Telling someone it's a dairy lunch day when it is really a meat day
- Using fake money
- Taking someone's belongings and saying that they're yours
- Telling someone he's needed elsewhere and then erasing his work
- Spoiling someone's work and blaming someone else
- Telling someone you can do something he can't do, but you really can't either
- Someone is looking for something and you see it but make believe you didn't
- Teaming up against someone in gym
- Telling someone the wrong rules for a game in gym
- Cheating against someone who doesn't know the rules
- Tripping someone who is running after a ball
- Telling someone that the next day the game will be soccer, but it's really baseball and he leaves his glove home

- When you don't want someone in your game and you tell him the teacher wants him

- When a group of friends decides to trick someone by saying, "jump" and none of them jumps except the other person

- Making cliques or groups and leaving people out

- Laughing at someone who is "clueless"

- Making fun of someone who has a disease

- Tying someone's laces together

- Selling something that doesn't work

- Telling someone he's your best friend but not meaning it

- Giving someone food you know he is allergic to

- Giving someone the wrong medicine

- If the nurse asks you how you are feeling and you say, "Terrible," when you are really feeling fine

- Asking someone to tell you his grade and then not telling him yours

- Telling someone you got a higher score than he did (when you really didn't)

- When someone "April fools" someone

Outside of School

For **Step #3**, the students also made a list of wrong behaviors outside of school. Here are some of their suggestions:

- Telling someone who is sleeping late that there is school when there really isn't

- Telling someone there's a secret passage in a closet and locking him in

- Telling someone you know is gullible something that isn't true

- Giving people the wrong travel directions

- Telling someone the diving board isn't slippery

- Holding someone down in the pool who doesn't know how to swim

- Telling someone he looks bad when he really doesn't

- Telling someone he has something between his teeth when he really doesn't

- Telling someone you will meet him at such and such place and you don't

- Telling someone he won a lottery but he didn't

- Telling someone the wrong time

- Tricking someone into eating non-kosher food

- Shaking someone's soda

- Saying bad words in a language the other person doesn't know

- When you're playing ball and someone tells someone to go back a base, and he does and gets tagged out

- Telling someone everyone will dress as a clown for Purim and then they dress as kings and queens

- Telling a little kid, "I'll give you two nickels if you give me one quarter"

- Selling damaged items

- Giving someone the wrong medical advice

- Putting cork in your bat at a home run contest

- Telling someone you have a super star's autograph when you don't

For the Student: What Would *You* Do?

Once, the grandchild of Rabbi Moshe Feinstein saw his grandfather pass by and he immediately ran over to him with several of his friends. Rav Moshe wanted to warmly greet his grandchild but didn't want to hurt the feelings of the child's friends. **What would you do in his place?**

Rav Moshe Feinstein, one of the most revered men of the twentieth century, renowned for his great Torah wisdom, bent down and kissed his grandson, and then proceeded to kiss each of his grandson's friends.

What Do We Learn from This Story?

We learn that:

- The laws of **Step #3** apply equally to children, as they do for adults.

- A great person thinks very carefully about even the slightest impact of everything that he does.

- Rabbi Moshe Feinstein was more concerned for the feelings of a small child than he was for his own *kavod* (honor).

Related Quote from Pirkei Avot

{
ובמקום שאין אנשים השתדל להיות איש

and in a place where there are no leaders, strive to be a leader (2:6)
}

We have seen how many different ways there are for people to mistreat others. Oftentimes, children feel that they must follow the "popular" students who sometimes set the wrong tone for the group. Although it can sometimes feel lonely, a good person tries to lead under such circumstances and encourage others to do the right thing. It helps to keep in mind that many good people are really hoping to see someone stand up for what is right.

If you have a story or personal success helping others avoid tricking or misleading others, please share it by sending it to mentschhood@gmail.com and putting "Step #3" in the subject line.

Step
·4·

פתח תפתח
את ידך לאחיך
לעניך ולאבינך
בארצך

**Open your
hand to your
brother, to
your poor and
to the needy
in your land.**

כי לא יחדל אביון מקרב הארץ על כן אנכי
מצוך לאמר פתח תפתח את ידך לאחיך לעניך
ולאבינך בארצך.

Since there will always be poor people in the land, therefore
I command you saying, Open your hand to your brother, to your
poor and to the needy in your land. (Devarim 15:11)

**"A mentsch is someone who knows the difference between right
and wrong and chooses the right thing even when it is the more difficult
choice to make." —Amy, teacher and parent of four**

Step #4

We have now reached the mid-point in the Seven Steps to Mentschhood. The three steps we have just completed require us to think carefully before we act, and often to avoid acting altogether. **Step #4** *is the time to remember that being a* **mentsch** *means not just thinking as much as it means doing.*

It teaches us that a mentsch knows the importance of giving tzedakah – charity.

What We Learn from Our Rabbis

One is immediately struck by the introductory phrase of the *pasuk*, which tells us that there will always be poor people in our land. This is an even more puzzling statement in light of a pasuk we read just a few verses before, which proclaims that there can be a time when there will be no poor among our people.

The Ramban tells us that the answer is in the previous pesukim (Devarim 19:4, 5). It informs us that the absence of poverty is conditional upon all of Israel following all the *mitzvot*. Sadly, because this is so difficult, the people of Israel are unlikely to achieve such an exalted state, and we will therefore always have poor among us. The Rashbam softens this judgment by quoting the pasuk in *Kohelet*, "For there is no man who is so wholly righteous on earth that always does good and never sins" (7:20).

Another question is asked: Why the double phrase פתוח תפתח (You shall surely open your hand)? Rashi answers that it is our obligation to give tzedakah to poor people not just once, but as many times as needed. We must also give charity according to the needs of the individual. If a wealthy person becomes impoverished, we must provide him with charity that more resembles his lifestyle than we would for someone who has always been poor.

Yet another question asked is the reason for the multiple languages for the recipients of our charity: "your brother, your poor and your needy."

Several commentators including the Chizkuni explain. The word אחיך, your brother, refers to those people closest to you, who come first. Then עניך – your poor – are the other members of one's family. Finally, אביֹנך, those of your own city. This hierarchy of giving makes it easier for anyone to apportion his charitable donations in an equitable fashion.

The *Admor*, *Sar Shalom* of Belz, suggested a novel way to understand this concept in *Iturei Torah*. He said that if one maintains a closed fist, all the fingers look to be the same height. However, when we open our hands, the fingers are of different lengths. Since we find the words לא תקפץ את ידך (You shall not close your hand) in another pasuk, we learn that we not only open our hands to the poor, but we also take into account their individual needs as well.

The *Malbim* also teaches us a meaningful lesson. He explains that since Hashem has made it clear that there will always be poor people, His plan clearly implies that there will also always be wealthy people. These people should therefore regard their wealth simply as a deposit from which the poor are entitled to withdraw. In essence, the wealthy man gives to the poor that which Hashem has entrusted to his temporary care.

Lastly, our Rabbis explain why the pasuk uses the word לאמר – as in,

"therefore I command you *saying* . . ." – This comes to teach us an important principle: גדול המעשה יותר מהעושה (Talmud Baba Batra p. 9), that the one who tells others to do the correct thing is greater than the one who simply acts on his own.

When asked why the Torah tells us that there will always be poor people, this was the answer of a fourth grader:

"Hashem made the world unfinished, and it is our job to finish it. When we give tzedakah to the poor and are no longer needy, then the world will be perfect."
—Areli

Combining
Step #1 & Step #4 = LOVE

Micha, the *Navi*, spells out a concise and beautiful formula for how we should conduct ourselves as Jews (Micha, 6:8):

> הגיד לך אדם מה טוב ומה ה' דורש ממך כי אם עשות משפט,
> **ואהבת חסד** והצנע לכת עם אלקך.
> Hashem has told you, man, what is good and what Hashem seeks of you: only the performance of justice, **the love of kindness** and walking humbly with your G-d.

What is the *pasuk* referring to when it says, *"ahavat chessed"* (love of chessed)? One answer is that, while it is meritorious to do acts of tzedakah and chessed, there are times that we perform them by rote and with little conviction. Here we are taught that our goal is to *love* to perform acts of chessed.

How can we understand this idea of love and chessed? In his book, *Twerski on Spirituality*, Rabbi Abraham Twerski, MD, describes a striking point made by Rabbi Eliyahu Dessler in *Michtav MeEliyahu* Vol. 1: "It is not that you give to those whom you love, but, to the contrary, you love those to whom you give." When you give tzedakah or provide chessed for someone, "you are actually investing something of yourself in him . . . and you develop a positive feeling toward any recipient of your chessed." As a result, Rabbi Dessler says, by engaging in acts of chessed we actually experience a greater sense of *ahavat Yisrael*, love of our fellow Jews.

Understanding the Mitzvah of Tzedakah – Giving Charity

Much of this section is based on two articles: "Tzedakah: Charity," courtesy of the Mechon Mamre website, http://www.mechon-mamre.org/jewfaq/tzedakah.htm and "The Inner Essence of Mitzvat Hatzedaka" by Linda Pardes Friedberg, published by Pardes Institute of Jewish Studies, September 27, 2000.

"Tzedakah" is the Hebrew word we translate in English as the word "charity." But these two words and their definitions reflect two different concepts. Charity usually denotes acts of generosity and goodwill that one performs for the poor and the needy. While we also feel this way when giving tzedakah, the word actually comes from the Hebrew root *tzadi-daled-kuf*, which refers to *tzedek* – justice or fairness. It isn't just a question of being nice to our fellow man that inspires us to give tzedakah, it is also a duty that each of us must perform on behalf of our fellow man.

Most of us recall that on the holiest days of the year – Rosh Hashanah and Yom Kippur – during one of the holiest our prayers, *Unetaneh Tokef,* we recite the sacred formula for deliverance from our transgressions: "*teshuva, tefilah, tzedakah.*" One can readily understand why we speak of prayer and repentance at this time, but why single out the mitzvah of tzedakah? The answer would seem to be that as we petition Hashem to be charitable to us and inscribe us for a good year, we try to emulate this behavior that He holds so dear, by making our pledge to provide charity for his creatures. The Chafetz Chaim quotes the *pasuk* in Micha (7:18), ...כי חפץ חסד הוא (A desirer of chessed is He). As Hashem holds acts of chessed in the highest esteem, so must we imitate Him and do the same.

How Much or How to Give?

Most of the *halachic* guidelines focus more on the way we give tzedakah rather than how much we give. The Torah states in Devarim (15:7), לא תאמץ לבבך (You shall not harden your heart).

When giving tzedakah we must give with our whole hearts. Even if we are suspicious of the person asking for charity, we must give freely, trusting in Hashem to serve as the true Judge. As the Talmud Baba Batra (9a) states,

> One who gives a coin to a poor person is rewarded with six blessings, but one who comforts him with words is rewarded with eleven blessings, and one who does both is rewarded with seventeen – the numerical equivalent of "*Tov*."

In her article, "The Inner Essence of the *Mitzvat Tzedakah*," Linda Pardes Friedburg asks, "What is really worth more to a poor person – our coins or dollar bills, or a renewed sense of hope and self-worth?" She quotes Rabbi Nachman of Breslov:

> "With happiness you can give a person life . . . There is no one to whom he can unburden his heart, so he remains deeply pained and worried. If you come to such a person with a happy face, you can cheer him and literally give him life. This is a very great thing."

There is a story told about Reb Shlomo Carlebach who, while leaving his shul one Saturday night, was approached by an African-American man who asked for a donation. Reb Carlebach responded, "I'm so sorry, brother, my Sabbath just ended and I don't carry money on the Sabbath. It seems that I can't help you tonight." "You already helped me," replied the man to Reb Shlomo. "You called me 'brother.'"

When someone comes to your door requesting tzedakah: Linda offers the following suggestions. (**Note**: Children should never invite strangers into their home unless their parents are present.)

- Greet them warmly and invite them in out of the cold or heat.

- Offer some refreshments.

- Look at the person in the eye and listen sympathetically.

- Whatever amount you give, do it with a smile and a blessing. Say that you hope Hashem will grant them all they are lacking.

- Accompany them back to the door with a smile and wish the person well.

A personal note: Each day, when I attend services at my shul, there are usually people waiting to collect tzedakah. Although I am saddened that they need to collect money for their livelihood, I am happy that I can put the money directly into their hands in fulfillment of **Step #4** *– "Open up your hand to your brother . . ." At the same time I eagerly anticipate the bracha I will receive for myself and my family that is almost sure to follow, and I gratefully thank them.*

Maimonides' "Eight Levels of Charity"

In his *Mishnah Torah,* "Laws of charity" (10:7–14), Maimonides – the Rambam – teaches us that there are eight levels of charity, each greater than the next:

(1) The greatest level is to support a fellow Jew by helping with a loan or by finding him a job so that he will no longer be depending upon others for support.

(2) The next highest level is the anonymous donor and the anonymous recipient. The donor does not know the person who will receive his charity, and the recipient does not know who his benefactor is. This charity is given solely for the sake of Heaven.

(3) The next level is the person who knows the recipient but the benefactor does not know who the donor is. Some of the sages of the past secretly placed coins in the doors of the poor.

(4) The next level down is the donor who does not know the recipient, but the recipient knows his benefactor. Some sages in the past packed coins in their scarves, rolled them over their backs, while the poor would pick the coins out of the scarves.

(5) A lower level is the person who gives to a poor person directly, *before* being asked.

(6) Still lower is the person who gives to a poor person *after* being asked.

(7) The next-to-last level is the person who gives inadequately but with a smile.

(8) The lowest level is the person who gives unwillingly.

A Story from Our Past

One of the most extraordinary men in all of our history was the noted British philanthropist and *ba'al chessed*, Moses Montefiore. A wealthy banker (and sheriff of London!), Sir Montefiore, as he became known upon being knighted by Queen Victoria, retired early and devoted his entire life to the Jewish people. He aided the Jews of Syria at age sixty-five, the Jews of Russia at age seventy-one, the Jews of Morocco at age seventy-eight and the Jews of Rumania at age eighty-four. It is noteworthy that Sir Moses was highly regarded by gentile kings and heads of state because of his activism on behalf of his people.

Moses Montefiore is best known for his devotion to the City of Jerusalem. Having visited the Holy Land several times, he was drawn to the holiest of cities. At that time Jerusalem was a crowded, impoverished home to many ethnic groups and religions packed into the Old City. No one could leave the walls of the city at night because of the great danger it posed because of thieves and highwaymen. With huge sums of money, Sir Moses began buying up tracts of land outside of the Old City. In 1860 a viable settlement known as *Mishkenot She'anannim* was established. Residents could work inside the city walls, yet have a safe haven for their families outside. Soon after, Sir Moses decided that he wanted to do more to help the Jews of the city become self supporting, and he built a windmill to grind grain into flour.

Sir Moses Montefiore lived to be 100 years of age, and this special birthday was celebrated by Jews the world over.

Another Story of the Chafetz Chaim

Paraphrased from *Love Your Neighbor* by Rabbi Zelig Pliskin, pp. 302–303.

When he was a young man, Yisrael Meir Kagan (the Chafetz Chaim) would often sleep in the *beit midrash* following his long hours of learning. To provide him with a modicum of comfort, his mother gave him one of their few possessions: a pillow. One day, his mother asked him to bring the pillow home so that she could wash it. The young Chafetz Chaim told her not to bother since it was already washed.

A short time later it became known that the maid of a local resident had married a very poor young man. In order to help set up their meager home, the Chafetz Chaim had given the couple his only pillow.

Lessons from These Stories

(1) It would be hard to overestimate the impact that Sir Moses Montefiore had on the City of Jerusalem and on the entire Jewish people. World Jewry learned so much from him. He taught us that we have a responsibility to Jews in need all over the world – that wherever we may live, we have a responsibility to support *Eretz Yisrael* and *Yerushalayim*. He demonstrated, by building the windmill, that we must strive to fulfill the Rambam's highest level of tzedakah.

We will never know how much Sir Moses Montefiore contributed to the rebuilding of Yerushalayim and to the eventual establishment of the State of Israel. Sir Moses Montefiore and his wife, Lady Judith, never had any children. But he will be lovingly remembered by all for his tzedakah and chessed for all time.

(2) There is not a lot to add to the story of the Chafetz Chaim's act of selflessness. Despite his discomfort from having to sleep without a pillow, he must have been pleased that his gift enabled him to perform the mitzvah of הכנסת כלה – providing for the bride.

Note: When discussing this story with my students, we often debated as to whether or not the Chafetz Chaim was wrong in not telling the truth about the pillow to his mother. Usually the discussions concluded with the decision that he told his mother the truth (surely he himself had cleaned the pillow before giving away as a gift) and that by adding more details he would unnecessarily upset his mother which he most certainly would never wish to do.

A Story Worth Noting

The Talmud Yoma (37b) tells us the story of *Heleni HaMalka* – Queen Heleni – who reigned in a kingdom north of Syria. She converted to Judaism after learning the Torah from Jews who passed through her kingdom. She frequently visited *Yerushalayim* and would bring gifts to the Temple. One of those gifts was a beautiful menorah fashioned out of gold to adorn the very top of the entrance to the *Beit Hamikdash*.

As you know, the time for the recitation of the *Shema* and our morning *tefilot* are determined by the rising sun. This was even more the case prior to the invention of the clock. At that time, there were many Jews who lived down in the valley whose view of the sunrise was blocked by the surrounding mountains. But when Queen Heleni's golden menorah was installed, the glint of the sun on its shiny surface was visible to all the people who would then know when to say the Shema.

The message of this story is clear. Like the gift of Heleni, when we give tzedakah, we never know how far-reaching the benefits of our chessed may be. A simple act on our part may bring bright rays of sunshine to the lives of the poor and downtrodden.

Learning to Apply Step #4 in School and Beyond

Step #4 represents the only concrete and hands-on activity on our road toward "Mentschhood." It provides children with a tangible opportunity to engage in a limitless number of actions they may undertake on behalf of others. It is hoped that through these activities, the practice of tzedakah and chessed will become second nature to our children. The key is the physical engagement on the part of the child.

William Glasser* has posited the following insightful analysis of the effectiveness of the various modes of learning:

---

* Although Glasser is most often credited with this insight, the quote more likely

We learn:

10% of what we read

20% of what we hear

30% of what we see

50% of what we both see and hear

And:

70% of what is discussed with others

80% of what we experience personally

95% of what we *teach* someone else.

Or in the words of the Chinese proverb:

I hear, and I forget

I see, and I remember

I do, and I understand

There is no tzedakah or chessed activity that is as meaningful as the ones we do with our own hands and even more so with those that we encourage others to participate in.

Tzedakah and Chessed at School

It is a pleasure to note that these days our yeshivot offer students a myriad of opportunities to practice **Step #4** in school. There is a preponderance of collections, drives and campaigns, all aimed at providing the students with personal, hands-on experiences.

In addition to setting a good example for their children and encouraging their participation in these events, parents can have a very meaningful role in the school's tzedakah and chessed programs. Here are a few:

Parents may

- suggest various causes and potential recipients to the school administration;

comes from Edgar Dale's *Core of Learning*.

- volunteer to help with the school's various campaigns and drives (this might include some of the difficult tasks associated with pick-ups and deliveries);
- offer to join forces with the PTA to hold some of these campaigns;
- join a parent group to work closely with the administration to recommend and organize special events.

It is very important for parents and school officials to maintain the hands-on, personal nature of these endeavors. While it is perfectly fine for children to bring tzedakah money to school, it is more meaningful when they perform tasks that are more memorable and can actually be life-altering. As we often hear from students and adults alike, while they don't remember much of the academic work they were taught in elementary school, many of the special projects and activities they participated in will never be forgotten.

Some Suggestions

(Where age appropriate)

- Nursing home visits where the children interact with the residents (This should *not* be the case when the residents are ill or too enfeebled to respond)
- Packing and delivering food for Tomchei Shabbat
- Bringing toys and other gifts to hospitals
- Serving the poor in a soup kitchen
- Volunteering to help children of parents who are ill or unable to adequately care for the family

Two Noteworthy School Projects

The following projects were successfully ongoing for several years at Westchester Day School in Mamaroneck, New York:

(1) **Chevrat Chessed:** A group of volunteer parents meet regularly with the school administration to plan hands-on tzedakah and chessed programs and projects. These parents do the research on

each project, supply classroom teachers with information to share with the students and arrange for collections and deliveries where applicable.

(2) **Talmidainu:** Volunteer parents seek out families with children whose physical or emotional disabilities prevent them from attending Yeshiva. They work with teachers – usually at holiday times – to create special activities for these children and the students whose classrooms they will visit. Most of the children invited to date have been autistic. These children become de facto members of the student body, hence the name, "Talmidainu."

Outside of School

The possibilities for tzedakah and chessed activities outside the home and school are limited only by the dedication and imagination of the parents and children. The most important factor leading to success is the role-modeling of the parents. Once children see that engaging in acts of tzedakah and chessed are a normal and regular part of their parents' lives, they are likely to adopt the same habits. It is also very helpful for parents to include their children in the planning of their joint enterprises.

A Noteworthy Idea: Birthdays and Chessed

Over the past few years, several initiatives have been introduced to merge birthday celebrations with act of tzedakah and chessed. Among them are the following:

- Having a child pick out one of his birthday gifts and donate it to a worthy recipient

- Asking guests to forgo a regular gift in favor of making a donation to a favorite charity

- "Twinning" with a child of the same age and sharing presents with him

There have been frequent stories over the years of children who have selflessly donated all or a portion of their Bar/Bat Mitzvah gifts.

Recently, a young man raised $18,000 in lieu of Bar Mitzvah gifts for a worthy charity in Israel.

Parents take note: If you train your children to look for opportunities to practice tzedakah and chessed, sit back and enjoy! You will be amazed at the results.

I enjoyed reading the following poem to my students and they enjoyed hearing it as well:

Everybody, Anybody, Somebody & Nobody
By Charles Osgood

There was a most important job
   that needed to be done,
And no reason NOT to do it, there
   was absolutely none.
But in vital matters such as this,
   the thing you have to ask
Is WHO exactly will it be who'll
   carry out the task.
Anybody could have told you that
   Everybody knew
That this was something SOMEBODY
   would surely have to do.
Nobody was unwilling. Anybody had
   the ability.
But NOBODY believed that it was his
   responsibility.
It seemed to be a job that ANYBODY
   could have done,
If Anybody thought he was supposed
   to be the one.
But since Everybody recognized that
   Anybody could, Everybody took for granted that
   Somebody would.
But Nobody told Anybody that we
   are aware of,
That he would be in charge of seeing
   it was taken care of.

And Nobody took it on himself to
   follow through
And DO what Everybody thought that
   Somebody would do.
When what Everybody needed so
   did not get done at all,
Everybody was complaining that
   Somebody dropped the ball.
Anybody then could see it was an
   awful crying shame,
And Everybody looked around for
   SOMEBODY to blame.
Somebody should have done the job,
   and Everybody would have,
But in the end Nobody did what
   Anybody could have.

An amazing fact!

The State of Israel provides aid to more than 114 countries, with some of whom it does not even have full diplomatic relations.

A Beautiful Story to Remember

(From *Chicken Soup for the Soul*)

Dan Clark tells the following story that took place when he was a teenager. He and his father were standing on a line waiting to buy tickets to the circus. In front of them was a family of about eight children along with their parents. One could tell they were very poor, and they were waiting with great excitement to have this very rare treat of a day at the circus. Their father was so proud to be able to provide it for them.

When he got to the counter, he told the ticket lady how many he needed, and when she responded with the cost his mouth began to quiver as he asked her to repeat the figure. It was clear that he didn't have enough money. He was crushed! How could he turn around and tell his family that he couldn't afford the tickets?

As he witnessed what was happening, Dan's father put his hand in his pocket, pulled out a $20 bill and dropped it on the ground. He then bent down, picked up the money, tapped the father on the shoulder and said: "Excuse me sir, this fell out of your pocket."

The man knew exactly what was happening. With quivering lips and a tear running down his cheek, he took the money from Dan's father with quiet expressions of deep and sincere gratitude.

Dan's father wasn't a wealthy man, and having given the family all the money he had, they simply returned to the car and drove home. One might expect Dan to have been sorely disappointed, but as one can tell, he was raised well. His comment about the event: "We didn't go to the circus that night, but we didn't go without."

For discussion: What did the author mean when he said, ". . . but we didn't go without"?

For the Student: What Would *You* Do?

The following two stories can be found in Rabbi Zelig Pliskin's wonderful book, *Love Your Neighbor*:

(1) A poor man once came to the home of Rabbi Boruch Ber Leibowitz to ask for a donation. Rabbi Leibowitz, who was very poor himself, did not have any money to give. As the poor man left his home Rav Boruch Ber accompanied him and they walked quite a distance. When Rabbi Leibowitz's disciples saw their teacher walking with the man, they joined him and it was very noticeable that the poor man was overwhelmed by the great honor being bestowed upon him. Afterward, Rav Boruch Ber explained his behavior.

Do you think you can figure out what Rav Boruch Ber said?

(2) Walking one day in Jerusalem, Rabbi Aharon Kotler suddenly turned around, ran after a beggar, and gave him some coins.

Can you figure out why Rav Kotler acted in such an unusual fashion?

(1) Rav Boruch Ber explained that a beggar humiliates himself when asking for donations. He said that even though he wasn't able to give him any money, at least he could give him honor.

(2) Rav Kotler explained that several years before this same beggar had approached him for money and he had none at that time. When he saw him this time he wanted to make up for the lost opportunity and gave double the amount.

In the case of both Rav Boruch Ber Leibowitz and Rav Aharon Kotler, we learn that great men shed their own mantle of honor on behalf of people who normally expect no honor at all. It is meaningful to note that by acting in this humble fashion, these two men of Torah actually grow in stature.

A Final Story: The Transforming Power of Tzedakah & Chessed

The noted psychologist Dr. David Pelcovitz tells this story:

There was a young, shy girl of about eight or nine years of age who lived in the working-class neighborhood of her town. One day she was encouraged by her mother to spend time with an elderly blind woman who lived nearby. The blind woman was upbeat about her condition and told her young friend that in two years she would be eligible for assistance and could undergo an operation that would return her sight.

The prospect of such a long wait troubled the young girl greatly, and the next day at school, overcoming her natural shyness, she told her friends and classmates about the lady and began soliciting funds. Surprisingly, her appeal was sufficiently moving and many of her schoolmates contributed to her cause.

Excitedly, she put the money in an envelope and proceeded directly to her neighborhood ophthalmologist. She told him about the woman and asked him to perform the operation. Proudly she handed him the envelope which he carefully opened. Inside he found eighty-three crumpled dollars. Touched by the girl's kindness and determination, he agreed to do the surgery. The operation was successful and the woman's sight was restored.

A short time later the young girl's mother learned of the incident. Although she was very proud of her daughter, she was nonetheless distraught over what she thought was an imposition upon the surgeon. She went to see the doctor and asked him to let her know how much the surgery cost so that she could repay him. The doctor told her that it wouldn't be necessary, and in fact, he told the mother that her daughter had actually done him a favor. He took out the envelope that had contained the crumpled bills and told her that he carries it with him all the time. He often takes it out of his pocket to look at, and to be reminded about how good people can be.

Related Quotes from Pirkei Avot

על שלשה דברים העולם עומד: על התורה, ועל העבודה, ועל גמילות חסדים.

the existence of the world depends on three things: on Torah study, on the service of Hashem and on kind deeds. (1:2)

These are the foundations of Jewish life. We must study Torah, so that we will know the proper path in life; we serve Hashem by following His Torah, and we perform act of chessed because this is the way we put Hashem's Torah into practice in our daily lives.

יהי ביתך פתוח לרוחה ויהיו עניים בני ביתך

Let your house be open wide; treat the poor as members of your household (1:5)

We learn from this *mishnah* that our home must be a refuge for all who are needy. We learn also that when there are poor people in our homes, they must be accorded the same treatment as members of our own family.

> אם אין אני לי מי לי? וכשאני לעצמי מה אני? ואם לא עכשו
> אימתי?
> If I am not for myself who will be for me? And if I am for myself, what am I? And if not now when? (1:14)

We are taught to take good care of ourselves. Yet if we only focus on our personal welfare, then we become self-centered. That is why we are also instructed to watch out for the welfare of others. We are also taught that we should not say we will act upon our good instincts only once we feel we are ready, but we must not delay in our dedication to helping those in need.

> ולא המדרש הוא העקר, אלא המעשה.
> not study, but practice is the main thing. (1:17)

While study is essential in order for us to know how to conduct ourselves, ultimately we are judged not on our scholarship but on how we put our learning into practice for the betterment of the world around us.

■ □ ■

If you would like to share an idea for a special school- or home-based tzedakah or chessed project, please share it by sending it to sevensteps@ mentschhood.com and writing "Step #4" in the subject line.

Step ·5·

ועשית הישר והטוב בעיני ה'

You shall do
what is right
and what
is good in
the eyes of
Hashem

ועשית הישר והטוב בעיני ה', למען ייטב
לך ובאת וירשת את הארץ הטבה אשר נשבע ה'
לאבתיך.

**You shall do what is right and what is good in the eyes of
Hashem**, so that it will be good for you, and you will possess the
good land that Hashem swore to give to your forefathers.

(Devarim 6:18)

**"A mentsch is someone who is not afraid to do the right thing even when
it is not the cool thing to do."** —Josh, grade 4

Step #5

Now that we have learned which behaviors are right and which are wrong, we turn our attention to a greater challenge: knowing when to do more for someone than we need to.

What We Learn from Our Rabbis

In the opening passage, the Torah tells us to follow carefully all of Hashem's commandments. Our pasuk tells us that if we follow those commandments by doing what is *right* and what is *good*, Hashem will bless us, along with the land He promised to our forefathers.

Surely, if a person does the right thing and follows the Torah and Hashem's commandments, then his actions will automatically be good. Why, then, are we asked to do what is *good* after we have already been told to keep the Torah?

The Ramban answers that the Torah cannot list every possible behavior that may arise among people. He notes that the Torah mentions several specific mitzvot regarding our obligations toward our fellow man (mitzvot *bein adam l'chaveiro*). For example, we are taught, לא תקלל חרש (do not curse the deaf [**Step #3**]), and מפני שיבה תקום (rise before an old person, Vayikra 19:30). Therefore, the Torah provides us with this guideline: just as one is taught to behave well in these specified instances, so shall a person behave in *all* of his interactions with people.

לפנים משורת הדין
Lifnim Mishurat Hadin

The second and related lesson the Ramban lists is the concept of *lifnim mishurat hadin* – going beyond what the law dictates. The Torah gives us many specific details of how the law requires us to behave.

Yet, there are times when a good person is motivated to do *more* than the law asks of us. The most cited example of this concept in the Talmud is found in Baba Metzia, 83a:

> Some porters [negligently] broke a barrel of wine belonging to Raba Bar Bar Channah. Thereupon, he seized their garments, so they went to complain to Rav. "Return the garment," he [Rav] ordered. "Is that the law?" he [Raba] inquired. "Yes," he [Rav] responded, "that you shall walk in the way of good people." (*Mishlei* 2:20)

> Their garments having been returned, they observed, "We are poor men, have worked all day and are hungry. Are we to get nothing?" "Go and pay them," Rav ordered. "Is that the law?" he asked. "Yes," he responded, "and keep the path of the righteous.'" (*Mishlei* 2:21)

The Talmud is teaching us that if a worker breaks his employer's merchandise, the law allows the owner to withhold the employee's wages. Yet, Rav instructs Raba Bar Bar Channah to refrain from punishing them despite the loss of merchandise, because he should go beyond what the law requires. He must act lifnim mishurat hadin.

The Talmud feels so strongly about this that elsewhere in Baba Metzia, 30b, it says that Yerushalayim was destroyed because its courts judged according to the strict letter of the law and not lifnim mishurat hadin.

This is the lesson of **Step #5**: You shall do what is "**right**" (*yashar*), and what is "**good**" (*tov*) – *beyond* what is right.

A Story from Our Past

Parshat *Vayeira* (Bereishit 18:1–5) begins with the story of *Avraham Avinu* as he sits outside his tent waiting for visitors to pass by so that he can fulfill the mitzvah of *Hachnasat Orchim* – hospitality to travelers. This occurs on the third and most discomforting day after his *brit milah* when, as one recuperating from illness, he is not obligated to perform such a mitzvah. In fact, the Midrash teaches us that in order to spare Avraham the strain of taking care of guests, Hashem caused it to be unusually hot early that day. Under normal circumstances, this would have made it unlikely for travelers to be on the road.

Yet Avraham's desire to do this mitzvah was so great that Hashem caused three angels to appear in the form of men. Upon seeing them approach, Avraham actually ran to greet them.

A Story from Our Time

On December 11, 1995, a fire broke out at the Malden Mills textile factory in Malden, Massachusetts. The owner, Aaron Feuerstein, was summoned to the factory, where he saw nearly his entire complex of buildings engulfed in flames. It appeared to everyone as if the factory would be a total loss. Aaron began to think of what to do next. As a seventy-year-old, he could simply retire on whatever reimbursement he would receive from the insurance company – he had no legal obligation to do more. However, more than his own loss was on his mind. He was thinking of his fourteen hundred employees who would be out of work, especially during their approaching holiday season.

Aaron Feuerstein, an Orthodox Jew, recalled the teachings of his father, who had run the factory before him. "A good name is the greatest treasure a man can acquire," his father had taught him. He also recalled his father's teaching from Pirkei Avot: "In a place where there is no man, do everything in your power to be one." Fortified with the teachings of his faith, Aaron Feuerstein decided not only to rebuild his factory, but also to pay his workers their full wages until the factory resumed production.

Aaron Feuerstein's behavior made headlines around the world. He was invited by President Clinton to join him at his State of the Union Address, where Aaron was given a standing ovation by both Houses of Congress. His behavior was recognized by the Jewish community as that of a true *kiddush Hashem* (bringing praise of Hashem from the general public). One newspaper headline declared, "All it takes to be a CEO – be a *mentsch*."

In one of his numerous television interviews, Mr. Feuerstein was asked what guided his behavior. He answered that a person must always do "what is right and what is *good*." He also quoted Rabbi Hillel twice in one of his interviews: "In a situation where there is no righteous person, try to be a righteous person," and, "Not all who increase their wealth are wise."

Lessons from These Stories

Avraham Avinu was not required by the law to perform the mitzvah of *hachnasat orchim* because he was recuperating from his *brit milah*. Yet his desire to be helpful to others was far greater than his concern for his personal comfort. Responding to such selfless desire, Hashem sent him the three guests. Avraham was truly acting lifnim mishurat hadin, *beyond* what the law required.

Aaron Feuerstein would have been well within the bounds of appropriate behavior if he had closed Malden Mills for good and offered no compensation to his employees. By putting his employees' interests ahead of his own, he too, was acting lifnim mishurat hadin. He went from doing the right thing to doing what we can call the *"better-*than-right thing."

What Yeshiva Students Said about Aaron Feuerstein

What he could have done:

- He could have retired

- He could have just forgotten about the factory

- He could have started a new (and easier) life

- He could have collected all the insurance (and taken off!)

What he did:

- He rebuilt the factory

- He paid his workers their full salary (for the time they couldn't work)

- He didn't retire because he cared about his people

- He displayed a nice attitude. He was very considerate

- He was a mentor (example) for other owners

- He didn't boast

- He did a *Kiddush Hashem* (sanctification of G-d's name).

Another Story of the Chafetz Chaim:

Once, someone stopped the *Chafetz Chaim* and asked him if he would change a large bill. When he took out his wallet, the inquirer grabbed the wallet and ran off. The *Chafetz Chaim* did what everyone would do under the circumstances, he ran after him. However, unlike (probably) anyone else, he did not run after him to recover his money. He did not say, "Stop thief!" Incredibly he ran after him yelling, "I am *mochel* you! (I forgive you!) and I absolve you of the obligation to repay." The *Chafetz Chaim* was so concerned that the person would be given the very serious label of robber, that he was willing to forfeit his money.

This is an extraordinary example of acting *lifnim mishurat hadin*.

Learning to Apply Step #5 in School

Walking into the classroom during recess time, a third grader found several of the boys teasing one of their classmates about his obesity. He was terribly troubled about his friend's feelings and he knew he should do something to help, but wasn't sure what the best approach would be. He was sure that if he reprimanded the boys they would tell him to mind his own business, or worse still – make fun of *him*.

He agonized over the situation for a few moments and then came up with a plan. If he could just create a diversion and draw their attention away, they just might stop what they were doing. Perhaps, he thought, I can speak with them about it when things are calmer. He quickly and loudly called the boys to his knapsack and showed them his new video game. Much to his relief, the plan worked and they stopped ridiculing his friend.

As we learned in **Step #1,** the boy in this story faced something that each and every one of us faces daily – the fact that we all must constantly make **choices**. From what we choose to wear in the morning, to what we eat for lunch, to how carefully we pay attention in class to how we treat everyone with whom we are in contact, we must make hundreds of choices each day.

How We Make Choices Is an Important Measure of Our Mentschhood!

The Four Choices

When we observe behavior that is anti-social, exclusive, hurtful, aggressive or abusive, we usually have **four choices**. What are the four choices the third grader faced when he was confronted with the other boys' misbehavior?

(1) There's the **wrong** choice – There can be many wrong choices. In this case it could mean joining the boys who were making fun of the overweight classmate. People often opt for this choice since they feel better if someone else is being teased. This means that they can be safe for a while.

(2) There's the **neutral** choice – Doing nothing and thinking to himself, "At least *I'm* not being mean to him."

(3) There's the **right** choice – In this case, it could mean telling the boys that they were doing the wrong thing. Perhaps he could add that they were going against the Torah and even tell them that they should feel ashamed of themselves. Yet this might not be the best approach. The problem with this choice, as the boy already realized, is that most of the time, children don't like to be lectured to by other children. In fact they often take their annoyance out on the person delivering the message. Clearly there are many cases in which the "right" choice might not really be the best choice after all.

(4) There's the **better-than-right** choice – In this case we might say that the boy chose the better-than-right approach. Although it was more difficult for him than making the **right** choice, his efforts brought about a favorable solution for his friend and left open the possibility of helping the others improve their behavior as well. **(Step #2)**

What About Tattling?

{ לא תלך רכיל בעמיך

You shall not go about as a talebearer among your people (Vayikra 19:16)

Sometimes when students see someone doing something wrong, they feel that they must immediately tell the teacher or some authority figure about it. In these situations, it is very important to remember the rules regarding *lashon hara* (see **Step #2**) and *richilut* – talebearing.

As a general rule, "telling on someone" is wrong, especially if one just wants to get the other "in trouble." When a student sees another student doing the wrong thing, his first obligation is to try to stop it on his own. Only if the person doing the wrong thing is likely to hurt someone, be it physically or emotionally, is it proper to tell on him.

There is really no place for a "tattletale" in the classroom or in life. Adults must be very careful to avoid abusing the trust of children by asking them to "tell" on their peers without very strong justification.

Everyday Examples in School

The following are frequently recurring events to which we may apply the lesson of **lifnim mishurat hadin**. (Note: These are examples provided by yeshiva students. They do not represent the only solution but are suggested guidelines. Remember, there are many cases in which the "right" choice may not really be the best choice after all.)

- Someone gets a low score on a math test:
  Right – Say to the person, "That's OK, you'll do better next time."
  Better than right – Offer to explain the work to him.

- Someone fails a test:
  Right – Offer to explain the work to her.
  Better than right – Sit with the person and do a page of the work with her.

- A new student in class is being ridiculed:
  Right – Ask the rest of the kids to imagine what it would be like if *they* were new.

    Better than right – Introduce him to some of the nicer students in the class who might be more receptive to befriending him.

- Someone takes a really awful shot in a basketball game, and everyone yells, "You stink!"
  Right – Ask everyone how they would feel if it happened to them.
  Better than right – Help him learn to master that particular shot.

- Someone does a problem on the board and gets it wrong and everyone laughs at her:
  Right – Tell everyone to stop laughing.
  Better than right – Wait till the person leaves the room and then tell them not to do it.

- Someone makes a reading mistake:
  Right – Correct the person.
  Better than right – Review the reading with the person in private.

- Someone takes something from someone and doesn't admit it:
  Right – Tell the teacher.
  Better than right – first try to get him to give it back.

- Everyone has to work with a partner and no one wants to work with a certain student:
  Right – Pick that person as your partner.
  Better than right – After picking her and working with her, tell her you enjoyed working with her and would like to do it again.

- Someone trips and falls and people make fun of him:
  Right – Get them to stop.
  Better – Rush over to help him up and ask if he's OK.

- Someone is not paying attention, and the teacher calls on him. He gets the wrong answer and everyone laughs at him:
  Right – Yell at everyone to stop laughing.
  Better than right – As soon as you can, go over and console him.

- Someone can't find a book in the library:
  Right – Direct him to the librarian.
  Better than right – Find the book for him.

- Someone makes a bad play in gym and her teammates yell at her:
  Right – Tell them they are wrong.

Better than right – Get them to stop by distracting them.

- Someone tries really hard to be on the basketball team and doesn't make it:
  Right – Tell him he's really good and will make it next year.
  Better than right – Help him become the team manager or scorekeeper.

- Someone wants to win the Presidential Physical Fitness Test but fails to score high enough:
  Right – Tell him he will do better next time.
  Better than right – Offer to help him practice some of the skills.

- Someone is being teased:
  Right – Tell them it's not nice.
  Better than right – Ask the person if she wants to play a game with you.

- Someone forgets his snack:
  Right – Give him some of yours and say he can give some back the next day.
  Better than right – Just share your snack.

- If students are working in a group and someone in the group always disagrees with the rest of the members:
  Right – Tell the person to try and agree.
  Better than right – Take the person aside and teach him how to compromise.

- Someone wants to sit at a certain table in the lunchroom and the people there don't want her:
  Right – Tell the people she has a right to sit there.
  Better than right – Ask the person to sit with you.

- Someone drops a tray in the lunchroom and everyone applauds and yells, "mazal tov!"
  Right – Tell everyone to stop.
  Better than right – Hurry over and help him pick everything up.

- Someone suddenly gets sick and throws up, and everyone says, "ewwwww!!!"
  Right – Find the teacher quickly.
  Better than right – Quickly help him to the bathroom or the nurse.

- Someone is sick at home:
  Right – Call and wish her a *refuah shleimah*
  Better than right – Review the work she missed on the phone.

- Someone's science project breaks apart:
  Right – Tell the person, "It's OK, you had fun anyway."
  Better than right – Ask the person, "Do you want help in putting it back together?"

- Someone spills something on someone else:
  Right – Tell the person not to worry, it will come out in the wash.
  Better than right – Get some paper towels and help the person clean up.

- Someone really messes up his work in art class:
  Right – Tell him not to worry, not everyone is an artist.
  Better than right – Tell him to meet you for a few minutes before class starts so you can show him how to do it correctly.

- Someone who usually does well in Chumash class does poorly on a test:
  Right – Tell him that everyone has an off day.
  Better than right – Offer to review the work with him.
  Really **better than right** – Ask him to review the work with YOU!

A True Story

A popular member of a class was invited to a party and two of his friends were not:

He could have – Asked them to invite his friends or tell his friends he will invite them to his own party.

Instead – He didn't go to the party out of solidarity with his friends.

An Important Tip

Why isn't it enough to tell someone who is doing the wrong thing to stop doing it? After all, we learned in **Step #2** that we are supposed to inform someone of his wrongdoing. While this remains correct, the fact is, that this approach often doesn't work. There are a few reasons for this:

- No one, neither child nor adult, wants to be lectured to. When a child feels he is being lectured to by a peer his first reaction is, "Who do you think you are?" or "Mind your own business!"

- Most people also do not appreciate being criticized or corrected in public.

- The person doing the correcting will be seen as a "goody-goody" and will have an increasingly difficult time fitting in with his friends and classmates.

Therefore, as we can see in the above examples, there are often better ways to correct someone without making even more trouble for one-self, and to prevent making things worse. Nevertheless, if someone finds that the only way to deal with the situation is to tell the person he is doing the wrong thing, follow these guidelines (similar to an "I" message):

- Never correct someone in front of anyone else. (Try recess or snack time.)

- Address the person by name.

- Try to be friendly and avoid the appearance of being better than the person or "talking down" to him.

Even if this approach doesn't seem to work, in many cases things will get better after a few low-key reminders.

For the Student: What Would You Do?

Story paraphrased from "Can I use Milk Instead of Wine?" in *Learning for Life*, an e-publication of Yeshivas Orchos Chaim, Pesach 5765. http://www.orchos.org/torah/chagim/pesach/pesachwine.html

(1) A poor man once came to the Brisker Rav on *erev Pesach* and asked the following question: Is it permissible to use milk instead of wine for the *arba kosot* (four cups) on *Pesach?* If you were the Rav, you would certainly know that one must use wine and not milk.

As the Rav, what would you tell the poor man?

Well, the right thing to do would be to answer the poor man's question and tell him that he may not use the milk. Can you think of another response?

Here is what the Brisker Rav did: He didn't reply at all. He took five rubles from his pocket and gave it to the poor man. Later, his wife asked him why he gave the man five rubles when only one would have been more than sufficient for wine. The Rav answered: "If he asked about drinking milk, then it was clear that that he had no meat either. I gave him enough for both wine and meat."

The Brisker Rav had done four things *lifnim meshurat hadin:*

(1) He didn't answer so as to avoid making the man feel uncomfortable or embarrassed.

(2) He didn't ask him if he needed either wine or meat.

(3) He gave him a sum of money that would have been more than sufficient for the man and his family to have an enjoyable *seder* meal.

(4) He protected the man's honor.

Did you decide you would do what the Brisker Rav did? The chances are that you didn't. But remember, the great Brisker Rav was once a small boy who also needed to learn to perform **Step #5**. Perhaps someday you, too, will be a great Jew who will teach much wisdom and kindness by the way you treat others.

The following story is paraphrased, based on the article, "Love Your Neighbor" by columnist Sheila Segal. http://www.ou.org/shabbat_shalom/article/love_your_neighbor/

(2) There was a family named Aaron consisting of the parents and eight children that lived in an apartment in Yerushalayim. One day the family decided that it was time to have air conditioning installed. They called a highly recommended contractor who told them that the best and most efficient place to install the unit was off the utility porch next to the bathroom. They agreed and in a couple of weeks the unit was installed.

That summer was one of the hottest in memory. The family was thrilled to have its wonderful new air conditioning unit working so well to keep them cool. The hot weather continued all the way through September, and at *Sukkot* time they got a knock on the door. It was from the downstairs neighbor who said that they could no longer stand the racket the air conditioner was making and they insisted that they had to get rid of it.

As it happens, the Aarons' neighbor's children were very noisy and repeatedly woke everyone up on Shabbat afternoon with their loud play. When the Aarons complained, the neighbors said they would try to do something about it, although nothing ever changed. It forced the Aarons to close their windows on very hot days, which was one of the reasons they got the air conditioning in the first place.

However, the Aarons felt badly about their air conditioner causing a problem for their neighbors and they called the expert back to tell him about their problem. The expert told them that he had installed hundreds of the same units and never got a single complaint.

What Would *You* Do?

The Aarons, nonetheless, insisted on moving the air conditioner even though the expert told them that it would be costly and it would reduce the efficiency of the unit. The new installation would also jut out into the space of their sunny porch. They told him to go ahead and a few hours and many *shekalim* later, the job was done. The children were very upset because they said that the air conditioner was ugly to look at and that they would constantly bang their heads on it.

However, Mr. Aaron surprised everyone when he said, "To me, it's beautiful." His stunned children asked how he could say that since the whole incident was costly and unpleasant and resulted in an eyesore.

Their father answered, "Yes, it's beautiful!" he repeated emphatically. "We didn't have to move the air conditioner. We weren't obligated by *halacha*. Our behavior is **lifnim mishurat hadin**. Every time I see that unit on the porch, it won't upset me. On the contrary, it has now become an object of infinite value, since we elevated it to **the status of a mitzvah**."

Related Quotes from Pirkei Avot

הוו מתונים בדין

Be deliberate in judgment (1:1)

The sages teach us to be very careful about how we judge others. Before deciding that someone has done the wrong thing, we must take into careful account all of the details and circumstances involved. Only then can we take action.

ובמקום שאין אנשים השתדל להיות איש.

in a place where there are no leaders, strive to be a leader. (2:6)

We return to this *mishnah*, cited in **Step #3.** There are so many times that we make choices each day. Some of those choices are difficult because we deal with people who don't always share our feelings and values regarding what is right and wrong. Correcting these people can be very uncomfortable and challenging. There are times when you might be the only one who knows the proper thing to do in a given situation, or who has a strong enough character to do what is right. Always try to be that person.

הכל צפוי והרשות נתונה. ובטוב העולם נדון, והכל לפי רוב המעשה.

Everything is foreseen, yet the freedom of choice is given. The world is judged with goodness, and everything depends on the abundance of good deeds. (3:19)

Even though Hashem knows the path that one chooses, we all have complete freedom to choose any path we wish. We should all aim to choose the path of goodness and good deeds, for the more goodness we bring to the world, the greater the blessings of Hashem. We should strive to follow the example of Hashem, Who judges for the good.

■　□　■

If you have a story or personal success in choosing the better-than-right choice, please share it by sending it to sevensteps@mentschhood.com and writing "Step #5" in the subject line.

Step
·6·

דרכיה דרכי נעם
וכל נתיבותיה
שלום

**The ways of
the Torah
are ways of
pleasantness,
and all its
pathways are
peace**

דרכיה דרכי נעם וכל נתיבותיה שלום.

The ways of the Torah are ways of pleasantness
and all its pathways are peace.   (Mishlei 3:17)

"Any citizen who is a good Jew is also a good American."
—President Harry S. Truman, 1953

Step #6

We have learned which behaviors are right and which are wrong and when we must even do more for others than the law requires. We now turn to an even more difficult challenge: learning how to do all of this with the proper attitude and spirit.

What We Learn from Our Rabbis

Step #6 is the only step that is not one of the 613 *mitzvot* of the Torah. It is a *pasuk* in *Mishlei* that refers to the teachings of the Torah. Our Rabbis teach us that the Torah's ways are pleasant and are not too difficult for us to follow. In fact, we learn from the *Ralbag* (Rabbi Levi Ben Gershom – Gersonides) that rather than being difficult and too challenging, the *mitzvot* are designed to be beneficial to us, both physically and spiritually. The *Metzudat David* adds that the Torah's "ways of pleasantness" prevent us from stumbling in our efforts to follow its guidance and laws.

The *Malbim* on our pasuk teaches us that the word *"derech"* in this case refers to the wide thoroughfares upon which all people travel, and that the *"netivot"* are the pathways of individuals. As we learn and are inspired by the Torah's "wide road," as individuals, we are inspired and fortified with the ability to take its lessons down the pathways of our daily lives.

What Is So Special About Pleasantness?

Clearly, there is something special about the concept of pleasantness, as it is inextricably connected with living our lives according to the *mitzvot* of the Torah. **Step #6** teaches us that as the Torah's ways are pleasant, so should we be pleasant in the way that we lead our daily lives and interact with others.

The Merriam Webster Online Dictionary defines pleasantness as follows: "Having qualities that lead to pleasure." The challenge of **Step #6** is to perform all the steps we have learned so far in ways that bring pleasure to others. We have all had experiences with people who act in a haughty and condescending fashion regarding the practice of their faith. We sometimes refer to these people as "holier than thou." A mentsch is someone who always strives to live and demonstrate his "yiddishkeit" in a pleasant and peaceful manner.

A Noteworthy Story

Rabbi Pesach Krohn, the renowned storyteller and author, relates the story of a man whose wife was in labor, who sped through the toll booth at the Brooklyn Battery Tunnel to get her to Mount Sinai Hospital as quickly as possible. A policeman stopped him on the other side of the tunnel long enough to hear the man's story and he then sped off.

Upon his return home after the safe birth of his child, the man offered the toll collector two tokens. When he saw the coins the toll collector asked, "What did you have – a boy or a girl?" The surprised man asked, "How did you know who I was?" The toll collector answered, "The policeman told all the toll collectors that an Orthodox Jew would soon come by and will surely pay for his earlier trip."

What Do We Learn from This Story?

The policeman had obviously had many encounters with Orthodox Jews and learned to see them all as scrupulously honest. Therefore, although he had never seen this man before, he simply knew that he would not fail to pay his fare. This phenomenon is referred to as a "kiddush Hashem" – the sanctification of Hashem's name, as we mentioned in the previous Step. It is for this reason that when someone fails to follow the "path of pleasantness" in public by not following the Torah's guidelines, it is referred to as a "chillul Hashem" – a desecration of Hashem's name.

Kiddush Hashem

We read in *parshat Emor* (Vayikra 22:32):

{
ולא תחללו את שם קדשי ונקדשתי בתוך בני ישראל
You shall not desecrate My Holy Name; rather, I should
be sanctified among the children of Israel
}

When a Jew acts in a way that causes someone to say, "How could a religious person behave so despicably?" it may actually cause an observer to question the very existence of G-d. This is a *chillul Hashem* (a desecration of Hashem). Conversely, when a Jew acts in a way that causes an observer to say that the only way a person could behave in such a fashion is if he were taught by Hashem, this is a *kiddush Hashem* (a sanctification of Hashem).

The Talmud Yoma (86a) explains the concept of *kiddush Hashem*. If someone learns Torah and is connected to Torah scholars and his dealings with people will be conducted in a **pleasant** manner, people will remark, "Praiseworthy is the person who studies Torah. Praiseworthy is the father who taught him Torah, praiseworthy is his Rebbe who taught him Torah . . ."

Do you recall the story of Aaron Feuerstein in **Step #5**? It was said that his behavior created a great *kiddush Hashem.* Mr. Feuerstein was accorded many honors at that time, including one by the Union of Orthodox Jewish Congregations of America. It was there that his Rabbi quoted the following story from Talmud *Yerushalmi Baba Metzia* 2:5.

It is the story of Rav Shimon Ben Shetach, whose students bought a donkey for him from an Arab. They discovered that a precious stone had been attached to the donkey without the seller's knowledge. When questioned why it was necessary to return the stone even though the law did not require it, Rav Shimon Ben Shetach answered that his goal in life was not to amass wealth but to a hear the non-Jew say, "Blessed is the G-d of Shimon Ben Shetach, blessed is the G-d of the Jews."

Both Rabbi Shimon Ben Shetach and Aaron Feuerstein acted *"lifnim meshurat hadin"* (**Step #5**), and both created a *kiddush Hashem* in the process.

It is important to keep in mind that we are not obligated to suffer great financial risk, or to risk our very lives to create a *kiddush Hashem*. As this gemara points out, the key is to strive to act in a **pleasant manner** toward everyone with whom one is in contact. Therefore, our goal is to strive to be the person about whom it is said, "Now there is a real mentsch!"

Hakarat Hatov (Gratitude Is an Attitude)

When our children are very young, one of the first things we teach them is the daily *Modeh ani* prayer: "I give thanks to you Hashem for returning my soul within me with compassion . . ." As they get older we teach them the *birchot hashachar* (morning blessings), when we thank Hashem for, among other things, our sight, our clothing, our freedom and even our ability to stand straight. In fact, by reciting all our *tefilot* and *brachot*, each day we offer 100 blessings to Hashem.

When discussing the mitzvah of *kibud av va'em* (honoring our parents), the *Sefer HaChinuch* teaches us that primarily we are obligated to honor our parents because they do so much for us. After all, they brought us into this world and they provide us with all our material needs. But the *Chinuch* goes even further: as we grow and make this trait a part of our character, we gain a growing recognition of Hashem's goodness, since He is the primary cause of our existence and for all the good that we have in our lives.

Two stories in the Torah help us better understand the trait of gratitude and recognizing the good. When our matriarch Leah gave birth to her fourth son, she named him Yehuda, a name derived from the Hebrew word for being thankful. The question is asked, wasn't she grateful for her other sons? Why did she wait to express her feelings of appreciation? Our Rabbis explain that the matriarchs knew prophetically that there would be twelve tribes. Since there were four matriarchs, that meant that each one would have three sons with Ya'akov. When Leah had a fourth child, she knew that she had received more than her fair share and therefore expressed her recognition of special gratitude for Hashem's goodness.

There is also another answer given. Leah was always envious of her sister, Rachel, whom Ya'akov loved more than he loved her. When she saw that she was blessed with her fourth son, she reconciled herself to her position in her family and was able to finally express her genuine feelings of gratitude to Hashem. Her actions represent an admirable level of *hakarat hatov*.

The second story relates to *Moshe Rabeinu*, who was hidden in the Nile River so that he would not be drowned by the Egyptians. Many decades later, during the first plague, when Hashem was about to turn the river into blood, He told Moshe to tell his brother Aharon to stretch forth his rod in place of Moshe. We are taught by *chazal* that the reason for this is that Moshe had a sense of *hakarat hatov* for the very river that saved him and Hashem knew that he would be reluctant to smite it.

From this episode we learn a remarkable lesson. The Torah teaches us that one may even have a sense of gratitude for inanimate objects. All the more reason, therefore, that we must be appreciative and grateful to all the helpful people we interact with on a daily basis. It is this daily recognition of the good that is done for us that is the essence of *hakarat hatov*.

A Story of Both Hakarat Hatov & Kiddush Hashem

Rabbi Pesach Krohn shares another story:

He was in a Canadian airline terminal and had walked all the way down the concourse to the very last gate where he waited for his flight. Suddenly he noticed that everyone around him was looking down to the other end of the concourse back toward the security area. Then he saw two security guards walking from gate to gate apparently looking for passengers. They drew closer and closer until they came directly to him. Feeling very self-conscious, he stood as asked, "May I help you, officers?" One of them held out a cell phone and asked if it belonged to him. He checked carefully and sure enough his phone was missing. When he realized the phone was his, they told him that he had left it in one of the security bins. He thanked the men profusely and told them how much time they had saved him from having to reprogram all of his phone numbers.

He then asked them how they knew the phone was his, thinking they recognized him by his rabbinic garb. Their answer amazed him: "Because you were the only one to say 'thank you' to both of us when you passed through the security gate. We would have looked everywhere for you until we found you."

What We Learn from the Story

Rabbi Krohn realized that while many thousands of people pass through the security gate, few if any of them ever thank the security guards. He felt that it was important to let them know that their work was appreciated. As someone clearly identified as a Jew to both the guards and the surrounding passengers, Rabbi Krohn was proud that they appreciated his noteworthy conduct.

One of my students once asked me to write a poem in honor of Earth Day. The result follows:

Earth Day Poem
By Stanley Fischman

Bereishit bara,
And Hashem saw,
that all His creations were good.
Some for the heavens,
for the land and the sea,
so that it would be understood;
That all that He did,
He did for us all,
to serve us as best as He could;
For each girl and boy,
To thoroughly enjoy,
And be thankful, as all of us should.

Thanksgiving – Giving Thanks

Those of us who grew up in or live in the United States of America are exceedingly fortunate. There are few places in the world, and indeed, throughout all of world history, that have permitted the Jewish people to follow our faith and traditions with as much protection and freedom. I have often told my students before the Thanksgiving holiday that we are fortunate to live in a country that devotes at least one day of the year to thank G-d for all He gives to us.

We attribute this holiday to the Pilgrims who observed the first Thanksgiving after an exceedingly difficult year, when they were on the cusp of starvation and many had died of disease. When they expressed their gratitude, it was not for the various dishes that were prepared for the feast. Actually, they were grateful to G-d for everything that He had blessed them with to ensure their survival. They probably recognized something that we, who are blessed with such abundance each day, might tend to forget: that all that we receive to sustain us is through the kindness of Hashem.

The Five Steps of Gratitude*

(1) Recognize all the good that you possess.

(2) Acknowledge that this is a gift, not something you are entitled to.

(3) Recognize the person who provided you with this gift.

(4) Recognize that the ultimate source is Hashem.

(5) Express your thanks.

An interesting thought: It's not the *challah* you are grateful for; it's really the mommy or *bubby* who baked it.

Another interesting thought: Think of the people you know who express their gratitude whenever they have the opportunity. Aren't these people also unfailingly **pleasant**?

---

* Based on an article courtesy of Aish.com.

A Special Message to Parents: Learning to See the Good

Too often, we as adults carelessly share our upsets, disappointments, anger and displeasure in the presence of our children. Have you at times found yourself speaking disparagingly or dejectedly at the dinner table regarding the state of the world, the situation in Israel or events in your community? While adults may understand that these exercises are release valves for our frustrations, our children take our pronouncements very seriously. This can sometimes leave them confused and frightened. It is therefore our responsibility to consider the sensitivies of our children when they are present during adult conversation and to make sure that "seeing the bad" is balanced by "seeing the good." For example:

- When we speak about some of the very serious issues that our brethren in Eretz Yisrael face each day, do we speak about the amazing things we have witnessed in the growing State of Israel – established so soon after the Holocaust? Do our children know that there are probably more people learning Torah in Eretz Yisrael today than at any time in Jewish history?

- When, tragically, a fire strikes a shul, do our children know about the firefighters – most of them non-Jewish – who risk their lives to save the *sifrei Torah*?

- When our children hear about people in our own communities who suffer financial or personal hardships or illness, do they also know about the myriad of chessed projects and programs that will swiftly and compassionately respond to alleviate the suffering?

Learning to "see the good" is a skill that both adults and children should acquire. We must be especially attentive to recognize the many opportunities we have to teach and to train our children to see the good that Hashem blesses us with each day. Let us strive to be that person about whom others will say, "He would rather light a candle than curse the darkness."

People who "see the good" are almost always unfailingly **pleasant.**

Performing Step #6 in School

> *"Rudeness is the weak man's imitation of strength."*
> –Eric Hoffer, American philosopher

Manners

Although striving to be pleasant is not always an easy task at school, there are relatively simple guidelines to help students achieve this goal.

Earlier I quoted the dictionary's first definition of pleasantness, which indicated that a pleasant person is one who provides pleasure for others. The second dictionary definition of pleasant reads, "Having or characterized by pleasing manners, behavior or appearance." It therefore appears that having manners is an effective way to demonstrate pleasantness to one's friends and classmates.

Having "manners" relates to habits and behaviors that demonstrate consideration to others. They are actions that make people feel appreciated and comfortable. We often refer to people who have manners as being "polite." These people show concern and regard for others. People with manners and who are polite add much to the pleasantness of their surroundings. The following is a list of some of the behaviors that demonstrate manners and politeness in school:

- Saying "please" and "thank you"

- Calling classmates by their first names and not just last names

- Letting others occasionally go ahead of you

- Choosing those who are not the "best" or most popular for your game or activity

- Picking papers off the floor even though they are not yours

- Treating food with respect at lunch time and snack time

- Not raising your hand and saying "oooohhhhh!" when someone is trying to answer the teacher's question

- Offering to share someone's heavy load of books or supplies

- Not looking at other students' personal belongings

- When you hurt someone, either physically or emotionally, try to say that you are "sorry" even if you feel you are not completely wrong

One of the most important examples of being mannerly and polite is finding opportunities to compliment people for their appearance or actions. This is not always easy for adults and children to do and we must train ourselves to look for these openings. People who are nasty and make hurtful comments and then try to cover it over by saying, "I was just kidding" bring unpleasantness to their surroundings.

A Story About Manners and Politeness in School

Early in the 20th century, Native American children were often educated on reservations in the western states in schools run by the United States government. The government agents would hire teachers – usually from the east – to teach in these schools. One of these teachers began teaching her students as she had been trained, and would follow up her lessons with questions. The students, however, would never answer. She kept trying, but without success, finally coming to the conclusion that these children were beyond stupid and she quit in disgust.

The next teacher did something the first teacher failed to do: learn form her students. When she noticed that the students failed to answer her questions, she strove to find out why. The answer gave her (and should give us) much cause for reflection. As it turned out, the culture of that particular Native American tribe frowned upon embarrassing anyone. Therefore, the students didn't want to raise their hand so that they would not shame their fellow classmates.

An Example Worth Noting

A group of junior high school girls gave the following note to their gym teacher:

> *Dear Mrs. _____,*
> *Happy birthday!*
> *Even though our grade is not perfect, you always*
> *try to improve it! Thanks for caring so much about us!*
> *Love, _____*

There are so many wonderful things to learn from this note:

(1) The students showed that they cared and were thoughtful by remembering and wishing their teacher a happy birthday.

(2) They showed her that they understood and agreed that at times their behavior could use some improving.

(3) They acknowledged that she had tried to help them behave in the proper way.

(4) They thanked her for her efforts, and especially for caring about them.

(5) They expressed their own sense of caring by signing their letter with "love."

Although I know that these girls wrote this note sincerely and without an ulterior motive, one would imagine that if a problem or a need arose in the future, this teacher would be very inclined to be helpful and supportive. She would be responding naturally to their thoughtfulness.

Smile and the World Smiles with You

In Ya'akov's bracha to his son Yehuda, he says, ולבן שנים מחלב – "and his teeth, white with milk" (Bereshit 49:12). The Talmud (K'tubot 111b) explains that when someone shows his teeth by smiling to his fellow man, it is better than giving him milk to drink.

Milk, which is associated with essential nourishment, doesn't compare to the warm feelings one receives when he sees a face with a warm, pleasant smile. As a leader of his people, Yehuda was given this *bracha* because it is fundamental to the way he must treat his people. It is also interesting to note that the plethora of portraits of our *gedolim* over the past several decades often show them smiling.

We learn in Pirkei Avot that one should greet people with a cheerful expression. Of all the manners and traits that we should cultivate, the smile tops the list. This is certainly true of the school setting.

There is also a related verse in Mishlei:

> לב שמח ייטב פנים, ובעצבת לב רוח נכאה
> A merry heart makes a cheerful countenance, but a despondent heart [causes] a broken spirit (15:13)

This pasuk teaches us that if a person has a happy spirit, it will be reflected on his face. However, the face of someone with a wounded spirit will reflect his inner sadness.

The cheerful countenance is best reflected with a genuine smile. Moreover, when someone is greeted with a bright smile, it brightens his life as well. Conversely, when we meet someone who is unhappy, his expression casts a dark cloud over our spirit as well. It is clear that a smile is a very important element in the lives of the ones who offer it as well as the recipients. The following anonymous portrayal offers additional, meaningful insight:

A smile costs nothing, but gives much. It enriches those who receive, without making poorer those who give. It takes but a moment, but the memory of it lasts forever. None is so rich or mighty that he can get along without it, and none is so poor but that he can be made rich by it.

A smile creates happiness in the home, fosters good will in business and is the countersign of friendship. It brings rest to the weary, cheer to the discouraged, sunshine to the sad, and it is nature's best antidote for trouble. Yet it cannot be bought, begged, borrowed or stolen, for it is something that is of no value to anyone until it is given away.

Some people are too tired to give you a smile. Give them one of yours, as none needs a smile so much as he who has no more to give.

Why Smile?

Dr. Mark Stibich, in his book, *Your Guide to Longevity,** offers several reasons for always cultivating a broad smile (paraphrased):

- **Smiling makes us attractive**: People are attracted by those who are cheerful and happy.

- **Smiling changes our mood**: When we are feeling down, we can give ourselves a lift by smiling.

- **Smiling is contagious**: Smiling helps other people feel more cheerful.

- **Smiling relieves stress**: When we are feeling down, the symptoms of stress that line our faces can make us look unhappy and overwhelmed. Smiling removes these characteristics.

- **Smiling boosts your immune system**: Smiling can actually help your body ward off disease.

- **Smiling lowers your blood pressure:** You can actually measure the drop in your blood pressure after smiling.

- **Smiling releases endorphins, natural pain killers and serotonin:** These make our bodies and minds feel good.

- **Smiling lifts the face and makes you look younger**: *We use far fewer muscles to smile then to frown.*

- **Smiling makes you seem successful:** Smiling conveys a sense of confidence to those with whom we interact.

- **Smiling helps you stay positive:** The more we smile, the more we tend to feel that things are going well for us.

There are many quotations that reflect the different attributes of a smile. The following are a representative sampling:**

- "The world always looks better from behind a smile."

- "A smile is the light in the window of your face that tells people you're at home."

---

* © 2010 Dr. Mark Stibich (http://longevity.about.com/). Used with permission of About Inc., which can be found online at www.about.com. All rights reserved.

** Authors unknown

- "If you smile at someone, they might smile back."

- "Everyone smiles in the same language."

- "The shortest distance between two people is a smile."

- "Wear a smile. One size fits all."

- "It takes seventeen muscles to smile and forty-three to frown."

- "A smile is a powerful weapon; you can even break ice with it."

- "Most smiles are started by another smile."

- "A smile is something you can't give away; it always comes back to you."

A Short Course on Human Relations
(author unknown)

(1) The six most important words: *I admit I made a mistake.*
(2) The five most important words: *You did a good job.*
(3) The four most important words: *What is your opinion?*
(4) The three most important words: *If you please.*
(5) The two most important words: *Thank you.*
(6) The most important word. *We*
(7) The least important word: *I*

Four Words that Saved the World

The following story was delivered to 1,000 members of the United States Army Chaplaincy by Rabbi Yossi Jacobson,* the first Rabbi to have this honor:

He was sold into slavery by his brothers, and thrown into jail for crimes he didn't commit. All of this happened when he was just a teenager. But Joseph (*Yosef hatzadik*) was not an ordinary person. Most people thrown into a dungeon with no realistic hope for freedom would be overwhelmed with fear and despondency.

Shortly after Yosef's incarceration, Pharaoh's butler and baker sinned and were thrown into prison and became his cell mates. In the morning, Yosef looked at the strangers and saw that they were sad. He

---

* Rabbi Jacobson is the Rabbi of Congregation Bais Shmuel of Brooklyn, NY.

immediately said to them, ‏מדוע פניכם רעים היום‏? – "Why do you appear sad today?" (Bereshit 40:7).

These simple words, offered as a demonstration of politeness and caring by someone who, by all logic, should have been consumed by his own self-interest, set into motion an extraordinary chain of events.

By having his dream interpreted, [the lack of] which was the cause of his anguish, the Butler eventually remembered Yosef to the Pharaoh, who elevated the young man to Viceroy of Egypt. In the years of famine that followed, Yosef was single-handedly responsible for converting the land into a veritable bread basket saving the entire Middle East and the world beyond.

Rabbi Jacobson went on to tell the chaplains that Joseph was a role model for them. He encouraged them to seek an opportunity each day to offer a greeting or a word of caring to someone who appears downtrodden. They may never know how far-reaching such a gesture might be. This lesson, of course, is applicable to each of us as well.

Conclusion

We conclude **Step #6** with the full text of the quote from Talmud Yoma mentioned earlier:

> We learn in a Braisa, "You shall love Hashem your G-d" [which can be interpreted as] the name of Heaven becomes beloved through you . . . as one's dealings with others should be conducted in a pleasant manner. What do people say about such a person? "Fortunate is his father who taught him Torah, fortunate is his teacher who taught him Torah."

> Rabbeinu Chananel adds the words, "Fortunate are his parents."

In today's language, when we encounter a particularly pleasant person, we are likely to say, "What a mentsch!"

Related Quotes from Pirkei Avot

> הוי מתלמידיו של אהרן, אוהב שלום ורודף שלום, אוהב את
> הבריות ומקרבן לתורה
> Be among the disciples of Aharon, loving peace and pursuing peace, loving people and bringing them close to the Torah (1:12)

Aharon, our first *kohen gadol,* was also famous for going out of his way to bring people together. By demonstrating love for his brethren, he served as a model of pleasantness and peacefulness.

> והוי מקבל את כל האדם בסבר פנים יפות
> and receive everyone with a cheerful face (1:15)

Regardless of our daily pressures, we should go out of our way to present a smiling, cheerful face. As the Chazon Ish said, one's heart is a private domain, and one's face is a public domain.

> והוי מקבל את כל האדם בשמחה
> and receive every person cheerfully (3:16)

A sour face is off-putting, but a cheerful face is infectious.

> הוי מקדים בשלום כל אדם
> [Rabbi Masya ben Charash said,] "Initiate a greeting to every person" (4:20)

Regardless of the demeanor of the people we come in contact with, be it friend or stranger, a cheerful greeting benefits both the greeter and the recipient.

■ □ ■

If you have a story or personal success in treating others in a pleasant fashion or demonstrating the Torah's ways of pleasantness, please share it by sending it to sevensteps@mentschhood.com and writing "Step #6" in the subject line.

Step
·7·

קדושים תהיו

You shall be
holy

דבר אל כל עדת בני ישראל ואמרת אלהם
קדושים תהיו כי קדוש אני ה' אלקיכם.

Speak to all of Israel and say to them: You shall be
holy – for holy am I, Hashem, your G-d.   (Vayikra 19:2)

"Frumkeit without mentschlichkeit is not yiddishkeit."
—Rabbi Moshe Gorelick

Step #7

*We have learned **Steps #1** through **#6** and we know how to treat others according to the instruction of the Torah. We now come to the last and the most difficult step: learning how to become "holy" people.*

What We Learn from Our Rabbis

Hashem commands all of us to be "holy." But what does this mean? On this subject, our Rabbis have much wisdom to share with us.

From early on, there was a difference of opinion among chazal as to whether קדושים תהיו – to be holy – was one of the 613 mitzvot. Many commentators explain the reason for this. Rashi tells us that it is not a specific commandment since much of the content of the Torah is contained within it. This can readily be understood by the fact that so many of the Torah's essential mitzvot are listed in this parsha. It is for this reason that the Rambam's definitive listing of the mitzvot does not include *"k'doshim tihiu."*

The Ramban explains further. The Torah warns us to be careful about certain specific, permitted behaviors – such as eating kosher food and interacting with members of our family – and to practice them in moderation. We are then taught the general rule of holiness. You will recall that in **Step #5**, we learned the rule of *v'asita hayashar v'hatov*, which teaches us the general rule of *lifnim meshurat hadin* – going beyond the requirements of the law. The Ramban is teaching us that k'doshim tihiyu is also a general rule; it teaches us that the Torah is not only concerned with our requirement to fulfill the mitzvot, but also, with the manner in which we perform them, so that they shape our character.

Rabbi Michael Rosensweig (Rosh Yeshiva, Rabbi Issac Elchanan Theological Seminary at Yeshiva University), in his article, "Kedoshim Tihiyu," further explains that the Ramban condemns those people who are scrupulously careful about the mitzvot but fail to follow the Torah's fundamental principles of how we must treat one another. Rabbi Berel Wein teaches us that the mitzvot are like stepping stones on the path to holiness. Yet careful observance alone is not a guarantee. It is the discipline associated with the observance of the mitzvot that creates the opportunity for character and spiritual growth.

As we come to recognize the significant challenge of becoming holy, a question can be asked: Why not simply remove ourselves from the challenges of daily living and cloister ourselves from its pressures? This notion is rejected by the *Chatam Sofer* and his son the *K'tav Sofer*, who remind us that this pasuk begins with the following words:

> דבר אל כל עדת ישראל
> Speak to all of the assembly of Israel

From this we learn that, on the contrary, the only way we may achieve holiness is by joining together. Rabbi Yissacher Frand very practically explains that there are so many mitzvot, that we simply cannot do them all ourselves. While we must focus on our own performance, we must also work on our relationship with our families and then with the broader society. Successfully observing all the mitzvot is a communal activity. The *Sefat Emet* adds that the holiness a person may see in himself is in, reality, a reflection of his membership in the group.

Let's turn to the rest of the pasuk. After commanding us to be holy, Hashem provides the rationale: כי קדוש אני ה' אלקיכם – "For I, Hashem your G-d, am holy." Rabbi J. B. Soloveitchik refers to this as the concept of *imitatio Dei* – the imitation of G-d. In halachic terms, והלכת בדרכיו (and you shall follow in His ways). As we learn in the Rambam's *Mishna Torah, Hilchot Deot, v'halachta* in this case means that we should strive to emulate some of His characteristics:

- Just as He is merciful – you shall be merciful
- Just as He is gracious – you shall be gracious
- Just as He is righteous – you shall be righteous
- Just as He is pious – you shall be pious.

However, as Rabbi Yisrael Salanter explains, Hashem is Holy in the heavens. Our task is not to be holy like an angel, but to be holy in our observance of those earthly mitzvot that are enumerated in the parsha, such as refraining from stealing, dealing falsely or lying.

The Kotzker Rebbe asks, "What does it mean for a person to be a mentsch?" He answers that being holy is "human holiness" (*mentschlichheilgkeit*), because the very parsha that starts with "K'doshim tihiyu" contains the longest list of humanistic laws in the Torah.

Rabbi Sampson Raphael Hirsch offers further practical guidance. He clarifies that learning to be holy results from a person's effort and discipline, and there are no guarantees of success. We are charged in the Torah to be holy through the observance of the laws. We are "people of holiness," not "holy people." On the other hand, Rabbi Jacob Rubenstein, of blessed memory (former Rabbi of the Young Israel of Scarsdale, NY) explained that if a Jew's behavior is disassociated from Hashem, he cannot be holy. We must strive to adopt His attributes and apply them to daily life. The *Sefat Emet* asks, "Why does the Torah add the word אלקיכם – "*Your* G-d"? He answers that Hashem associates Himself with what He calls a "גוי קדוש" – a "holy nation." This presumes, therefore, that even as mortals, we are capable of becoming holy.

Rabbi Saul Berman, Associate Professor of Judaic Studies at Stern College for Women and former Director of "Edah," asks how it is possible for someone to emulate G-d? We can understand the pursuit of holiness in shuls and in *batei midrashim*, but he believes that it is also possible to reach this state in our homes and places of work. We do so when we teach family members and associates to fuse concrete behaviors with concepts like loyalty, patience and tolerance in our speech and actions. Rabbi Berel Wein adds that we should strive toward holiness even when we are doing permissible things. It is reflected in the development of our personalities and can be demonstrated by simply being cheerful and optimistic. He adds that in a time when the concept of free speech has lost all proportions, we strive for holiness by watching our tongues.

As we develop a personality of holiness, we learn an important lesson from Rabbi Yochanan Zweig, Rosh Yeshiva of Kollel Beis Moshe Chaim in Miami. He said that right after the introductory pasuk of k'doshim tihiyu, the very next pasuk begins with the words, איש אמו ואביו תיראו, that a person must "fear" his mother and father. We learn from this that no sooner do we begin the task of making ourselves holy, than we immediately separate ourselves from our "self" and focus on our relationship with others. There are many among us, both children and adults, who tend to see themselves as the center of their universe. By following the laws of this parsha, we learn to focus on our fellow man.

In concluding this section, I turn once again to the Kotzker Rebbe. Quoting from the pasuk in Shemot (23:30) – ואנשי קודש תהיו לי ("You shall be people of holiness . . .") – he says that before the word *kodesh,* we find the word "person." The lesson is clear: First become a mentsch, and only then can you become holy!

Rabbi Yitzchak Adlerstein (Director of Interfaith Affairs for the Simon Wisenthal Center and teacher of Jewish law and ethics at Loyola University), in his article, "An Alternative to Disneyland Spirituality," writes:

> As Jewish parents, we are conscious of a different dimension in the education of our children than many others. We want them to recognize right from wrong; we wish to see them grow to become good and morally upright. But beyond this, we sense that there was a quality to Jewish life that kept our ancestors committed and upbeat about life when others wouldn't have survived at all. Jews knew holiness, or what it means to live as G-d's neighbors. We want our children to taste its delights.

Understanding Holiness

While our Rabbis have helped us understand the concept of being holy, it may still be difficult for some people – and certainly for children – to understand this concept.

When I teach **Step #7** in the classroom, I begin by explaining how I came to choose K'doshim Tihiyu as the final step. **Steps #1** through **#5**, although they increase in difficulty, are somewhat more concrete in nature. They teach us to apply specific actions to specific behaviors. The other two **Steps**, particularly **Step #7**, are more abstract in nature. Consequently, it is more difficult to apply these to our lives.

One way of explaining the notion of being holy to children is to compare the word "holy" to being "special." Rabbi Yosef Blau,

Mashgiach ruchani of Rabbi Isaac Elchana Theological Seminary at Yeshiva University, offers a unique perspective. Being "special," he says, is "The extraordinary way a Jew does the ordinary." Students are asked to identify behaviors that almost all people do but that Jews do in a very special way. Among the best examples are the eating of kosher food and the observance of Shabbat. While all people eat food and many people observe a day of rest, no other people engage in these activities with the same level of observance and intensity as the Jewish people.

On a more challenging level, we can point to the daily *avodah* – the way we pray to Hashem. Perhaps the best example is the prohibition of speaking *lashon hara* – gossip. While many cultures have rules against gossip, the Chafetz Chaim teaches us that there are fully thirty-one mitzvot and *averot* connected with this form of speech.

A Jew is "holy" when he strives to live an ordinary life in an extraordinary way through the observance of the mitzvot.

The following are examples of how some fourth-grade students understood the meaning of **Step #7**:

- "You take all the **Steps** learned so far and glue them all together."

- "You do all the mitzvot with pride."

- "It's the way you are connected to Hashem."

Here are some other noteworthy student insights:

- "Do things so you can be close to Hashem."

- "Do what Avraham Avinu did."

- "To be worthy of Hashem's miracles."

- "Hashem honors you more because you keep the mitzvot."

- [Hashem says:] "I'm your role model. Be as close to Me as you can – even though it's impossible – still try."

Name something that everyone does that we do differently:
"The way we treat Yasser Arafat [our enemies]!" —Josh

> *What does k'doshim tihiyu mean?*
> *"To walk in the path of Hashem."*   —Avigayil

Applying Step #7 in School

Nivul Peh

Perhaps the best way to learn how to perform **Step #7** is to select a specific behavior commonly found among children and convert it into a process of "extraordinary" self-improvement. For this purpose we will study the subject of ניבול פה – unrefined speech.

Definition: *Nivul peh* is speech that is characterized as profane or repulsive. It includes but is not restricted to the use of foul language.

Regarding the use of foul language or "dirty words," parents become quite alarmed when they hear this form of speech from children. This reaction, while understandable, is quite misplaced and unrealistic. We must, in fact, ask ourselves whether we have the same reaction when we hear its use by adults.

A few years ago a parent asked me to discuss the use of foul language among some of her child's fourth-grade classmates. I came to class armed with my lecture, ready to explain why young children often speak this way. I decided, however, to act like a teacher instead of a preacher, so I asked them to tell *me* why children use these words. As the students began to share their answers, I started to record their responses. Sixty-four (!) reasons (and described situations) later, I put my clipboard down and thanked them for how much *they* had taught *me* about this compelling issue.

 To sum up the results, the children made it clear that they hear foul language *everywhere*! There were responses that emerged from their contact with society: the television, videos, music, athletes, coaches, people in ball field stands, and scrawled on walls everywhere. There were reasons that were connected to peer influences: older siblings, influential friends, kids on the school bus, the desire to be cool, to be popular or simply to "fit in."

There were several responses that might be called "situational/emotional": getting hurt, being frustrated, being embarrassed, being frightened, being upset or angry, trying to hurt someone, losing something, etc. And lastly, it must be mentioned that children often hear foul language from the adults in their lives, including their parents.

In short, young children are no different from the vast majority of adults who use this language in precisely the same ways, and for the same reasons, on a constant basis. Naturally, just as with adults, these are reasons, not excuses. In the case of adults, they ought to know better. Regarding our children, they must be taught the difference between proper and improper speech.

As you discuss this matter with your child, the following suggestions will be of help in counseling your child to avoid nivul peh in school:

- Nivul peh can be seen as any use of language that could be said in a more refined way. When faced with a choice, it's always better to use the more appropriate word.

- Nivul peh refers to any words a child feels he would not want his teacher or parent hear him say.

- If one feels uncomfortable using a word, it should not be used.

- Chazal teach us the concept of *shomea k'oneh*: One who listens to (*lashon hara* or) *nivul peh* and remains silent (does not protest) shares the same guilt as the speaker.

- When parents hear children say, "Everybody does it," it is not enough just to say, "Well, we don't use that language in this house." **Step #7** teaches us to add various forms of the following sentiment: "In this house we aim higher."

- It helps to be reminded that the mouth we use for our *tefilot* should not be sullied by using inappropriate language.

Finally, in the definitions of *nivul peh*, we use the phrase "profane language." The opposite of "profane" is "holy." At school, the most practical way a child can aim to be holy is to use proper speech. However, children often feel that if they behave in a way that seems to be better than the way others conduct themselves, they open themselves up to criticism or ridicule.

While these fears are certainly justified in some cases, it is important to realize that the students who respond that way are in the minority. The "silent majority" of students in the class will admire such behavior and will more than likely learn to emulate it. Of course it is also helpful to remind children that **Step #7** – *k'doshim tihiyu*, being holy – is the most difficult step and, like any other difficult undertaking, we cannot expect to see perfection all at once. As the Torah teaches us, *"v'halachta b'drachav"* – You shall "walk in Hashem's ways" (Devarim 28:9). This walk has no immediate destination; it is a lifelong journey.

A Final Thought:
What (or Who) is Holy?

We learn the following in *Hilchot beit haknesset*, the laws of the synagogue: "One may sell a synagogue or other holy objects, *even a Sefer Torah*, to provide for [indigent] students or to marry off orphans . . ." The *Mishna Brurah* adds that the same is true for redeeming captives.

What an amazing concept! If people were asked to identify the holiest thing they know, most would probably say the Torah. Yet chazal teach us that this is not so. The holiest thing in the world is each individual. Every person is of inestimable value.

Each of us is *already* created holy. **Step #7** asks us to develop the behavior and attitude that complements our lofty status.

Related Quotes from Pirkei Avot

{ Be cautious with your words (1:11)

הזהרו בדבריכם

Wise people are very careful with everything that they say. They recognize that using the wrong words can have a strong negative impact on their listeners.

> איזהו היא דרך ישרה שיבור לו האדם? כל שהיא תפארת לעשיה
> ותפארת לו מן האדם
>
> Which is the proper path that a person should choose
> for himself? Whichever [path] is a credit to himself and
> earns the esteem of his fellow men (2:1)

As we strive toward being "holy," this portion provides us with an excellent road map.

> וכל מעשיך יהיו לשם שמים
> and let all your deeds be for the sake of heaven (2:17)

This, after all, is the reason we perform the Torah's mitzvot.

> כל שרוח הבריות נוחה הימנו, רוח המקום נוחה הימנו
> If the spirit of one's fellow is pleased with him, the spirit
> of the Omnipresent is pleased with him

Establishing this as our personal goal will put us on the path of *v'halachta b'drachav* – to walk in His ways.

■ □ ■

If you have a story or personal success in striving for holiness, please share it by sending it to sevensteps@mentschhood.com and writing "Step # 7" in the subject line.

Conclusion:
Moving Toward Mentschood

We have completed our study of the Seven Steps to Mentschhood. Followed carefully, they provide a solid set of guidelines for your children as you help them develop those behaviors and character traits that personify the kind of person we call a "mentsch." They are especially helpful in their application to your child's daily life in school.

In summary, while each step is different from the next and increases in difficulty, it is helpful to recognize the overriding similarity that unites them. A quick review reveals that six of the seven steps are *pesukim* from the Chumash. Of these six, five include a direct signature and message from Hashem:

> **Step #1**: . . . 'אני ה

> **Step #3**: . . . 'אני ה

> **Step #4**: . . . על כן אנכי מצוך

> **Step #5**: . . . 'בעיני ה

> **Step #7**: . . . אני ה' אלקיכם

The conclusion is clear: As we learned in **Step #7**, the principle behind the Seven Steps is the concept of *imitatio Dei* – to emulate Hashem and follow His ways.

Regarding **Step #6** – The pasuk, "The ways of the Torah are ways of pleasantness, and all it's pathways are peace" provides a broad guideline for "mentschlich" behavior. We can't expect a list of every possible way a person may choose to act in order to acquire Mentschhood; if, however, we follow the spirit of this pasuk, it provides us with a perfect path. Whenever you are faced with a choice as to how to behave like a mentsch in any given situation, just ask yourself, "What would Hashem say?" Once you get into the habit of asking this question, with the help of the Seven Steps, you will most likely make the right choice almost all of the time.

The Talmud (Brachot 25b) tells us: לא נתנה התורה למלאכי השרת – "The Torah was not given to the ministering angels." On the contrary, we must always keep in mind what we learned from the Kotzker Rebbe, who taught us that the Torah was given to men – ordinary human beings. Just as Hashem, in His infinite wisdom, created us with many talents and traits, He also created within each of us the capacity to follow all of His mitzvot, if we set our mind and heart to it. And just as no set of skills can be acquired instantly or easily (think of any sport), the keys to following the Seven Steps are continued and frequent discussion and review.

Parents are advised to encourage their children in the performance of these mitzvot and steps, and to reward them with meaningful compliments for specific instances of progress and performance. Ultimately, there can be no better reward for a child than to hear a parent say, "You behaved like a real mentsch!

A final definition: In our daily *"bentching"* (*birkat hamazon, Grace after meals*), we say the following: ... ומצא חן ושכל טוב בעיני אלקים ואדם

We ask that we may "find favor and good understanding in the eyes of Hashem and of man." (Proverbs 3:4)

A mentsch is someone whose character and conduct are appreciated by people and Hashem alike. This pasuk teaches us that when we concentrate on following the Seven Steps, and we consciously strive to emulate those traits that Hashem holds in high esteem, we will find favor in the eyes of the people who observe our behavior. It means that they are going to say, "There goes a real *mentsch!*"

Afterword:
Some Tips for Parenting Success

The following are some suggestions to help parents achieve success in their efforts at teaching mentschlichkeit to their children:

- **Consistency** – It is not possible for parents to always be right regarding their child-rearing practices and the advice they impart to their children. The key for parents is to strive to be as consistent as they can be in teaching their children their family's enduring principles. Children whose parents are consistent in their teaching will, over time, reflect their parents' values. Children are willing to give their parents much latitude for errors and slip-ups if, over the long haul, their parents demonstrate consistency in their teachings and their modeled behavior.

- **Honesty** – Each day we say in our prayers, לעולם יהא אדם ירא שמים בסתר ובגלוי, ומודה על האמת, ודובר אמת בלבבו – "A person should always be G-d-fearing, both privately and publicly, acknowledge the truth and speak the truth within his heart."

  Of all the behaviors with which we must be consistent with our children, one of the most important is that of honesty. And, as the *tefilah* dictates, honesty must start within the parents. The quality of honesty is not just for public display, it must be cultivated from within our conscience as a reflection of what Hashem wants from us. Parents who understand this faithfully model honesty for their children, whether it is convenient or not.

- **Integrity** – When our behavior matches our most cherished principles, we exhibit integrity. If not, we run the risk of appearing disingenuous or hypocritical. Children can easily see through such behavior. We must identify our most important principles and values, teach them to our children and always strive to model them ourselves. Integrity is the best way to teach our children right from wrong.

- **Elevating the child** – It is always helpful for parents to keep the following three points in mind:

(1) There is almost nothing that one might have to say to a child that could not be said in the same way we would say it to an adult.

(2) Everything we say to a child should be said in a way that builds his self-esteem, not in one that tears it down

(3) The most important message to convey to children when they do the wrong thing is, "That's beneath you," or "You are better than that."

- **Empathy** – is the ability to share in someone else's emotions, thoughts or feelings. In a presentation entitled, "How to Raise a Moral Child," Dr. Robert P. Granacher referred to empathy as the "bedrock of morality."

In Parshat Shmot, perek *bet*, pasuk *yud*, the Torah says regarding Moshe: ויגדל הילד – "And the boy grew up."

Just one pasuk later we read, ויגדל משה – "Moshe grew up." Why would the Torah need to repeat this seemingly inconsequential fact?

The answer lies in the rest of the second pasuk: ויצא אל אחיו וירא בסבלתם – "and he went out to his brethren and observed their burdens."

Chazal teach us that the first reference was to the fact that Moshe grew up physically. In the next pasuk, we learn that as he grew, Moshe went out and he saw the burdens of the people. We are taught that he saw their suffering and grieved with them. In short, Moshe grew in his ability to empathize with his brethren.

Oftentimes, when we point out the misfortunes of others, both adults and children are likely to feel sympathy or pity for them. Empathy implies the ability to put oneself in the other person's shoes. The ability to see the world through empathetic eyes is a valuable skill and one that will lead more easily to mentschlich behavior.

- **Modeling** – The most important element of effective parenting.

Seven Steps to Mentschhood

> *Parenting is difficult. But few things are more rewarding. Even if we are not great parents, our children are great children. My late father, z"l, who had little to leave his four sons, in fact left us the most precious thing that anyone can be given. He taught us, whether by words or just by being the person that he was, the values he cared for. He taught us the ideal he lived by. What he gave us was beautifully expressed by the poet Wordsworth in his Prelude* in a sentence that sums up the challenges of parenthood. He wrote: "What we love, others will love, and we will show them how." To teach our children what we love is not a small thing. Perhaps it is the greatest thing of all.*
>
> —Rabbi Lord Jonathan Sacks,
> Chief Rabbi of the British Commonwealth

---

* The full title is "The Prelude or, Growth of a Poet's Mind."